Mark Wasiuta
Akram Zaatari

Rifat Chadirji

Building Index

Mark Wasiuta
Akram Zaatari

Rifat Chadirji

Building Index

Rifat Chadirji

Building Index

Edited by:
Mark Wasiuta and Akram Zaatari

Design and color separations:
Tania Arwachan and Nadim Zablit, -scope Ateliers
English copy editors:
Anne Newman and Ros Schwartz

This book is typeset in Gothic 720 BT (Bitstream®).
The paper is Sirio Vermiglione, 290gsm for the soft cover;
Sirio Color Sabbia, 80gsm for the first 12-page folio;
GardaMatt Ultra, 115gsm for the inside pages.

Printed and bound by Brizzolis in Spain

First edition, 2018
Original print run of 1000

ISBN 978-614-8035-13-5

Cover page:
Akram Zaatari. The Fold, 2017 based on the building index of Rifat Chadirji

This building index is a part of the Kamil and Rifat Chadirji Photographic Archive, Courtesy of Aga Khan Documentation Center, MIT Libraries. It was digitally reproduced by the Arab Image Foundation, Beirut, in 2016.

The authors would like to thank:

Balkis Sharara and Rifat Chadirji.

Nora Akawi, Reem Akl, Florencia Alvarez, Zeina Arida, Vartan Avakian, Adam Bandler, Kristine Khouri, Ralph Nashawati, Walid Raad, Hashim Sarkis, and Roula Salamoun.

Sharon Smith and the Agha Khan Documentation Center, MIT Libraries.
Sarah Herda, and the Graham Foundation for Advanced Studies in the Fine Arts.
Dean Amale Andraos and GSAPP, Columbia University.

The Arab Image Foundation:
Co-director: Marc Mouarkech
Co-director and Head of Collections: Clémence Cottard Hachem
Archivist: Rachel Tabet
Digital coordination:
Charbel Saad
Digitization officers:
Christopher Baaklini, Mahmoud Merjan, Charbel AlKhoury

Published by:
The Arab Image Foundation and Kaph Books

المؤسسة العربية للصورة
Arab Image Foundation

Zoghbi Building, 4th Floor
337 Gouraud Street, Gemmayzeh
Beirut, Lebanon
Tel. 961 1 569 373
www.arabimagefoundation.org

KAPH

Park View building
Mina el Hosn, Solidere,
Beirut, Lebanon
Tel. +961 3 601 123
Fax. +961 1 999 068
www.kaphbooks.com

Distributed by:
Les Presses du Réel
(France, Belgium, Switzerland and Luxembourg)
www.lespressesdureel.com

Idea Books (rest of the world)
www.ideabooks.nl

Produced with the generous support of:
Graham Foundation for Advanced Studies in the Fine Arts

Graham Foundation

Additional support was provided by:

Aga Khan Documentation Center at MIT

Kurimanzutto (Mexico)
Thomas Dane Gallery (London)

THE UNINHABITED ARCHIVE 0294CH

Clémence Cottard Hachem and Marc Mouarkech
The Arab Image Foundation

Looking at the complex nature of fields of thought and activities that constitute archival practices, the Arab Image Foundation (AIF) situates itself within the modes of understanding the archive as a system of dynamic relations. The archive, never closed, fixed nor complete, is on no occasion a given. It is formed and constructed through an overlay of multiple interactions between collected objects and an array of physical and material interventions, along with questions of epistemological and ontological order, process, interpretation and use. The archive is thus perceived as being built through decision-making, conservation and transmission, through materiality, power relations and social concerns.

One might view part of the dynamics of the archive as its ability to be in *resonance*[1] with and to register in different contexts of handling, activation and reception as a an ever-changing construction. Also to be borne in mind is the archive's ability to feed thought processes and actions beyond its own system, to always question and activate its own properties and specificities. Due to the many visible and invisible strata that continually build the archive, due to the links that it cultivates and that underlie it, it remains open for elaboration. And this is precisely how it becomes a *resource.*[2]

Activating its photographic collections is embedded in the Arab Image Foundation's interest in exploring the dynamics of its archive, in enriching its semantic genealogy[3] while examining the evolvement of its significance through each activation.

In 2012, the entry number *0294ch* was given to the collection of The Chadirji Foundation at the AIF. This collection comprises documents assembled through various systems and practices produced and implemented by Rifat Chadirji and his team: a photographic practice documenting a disappearing Iraq, a documentary practice with undeniable ethnographic and anthropological potential. This practice was set in motion by a desire to witness and safeguard begun as early as the 1930s by Kamil Chadirji, and carried on later by Rifat Chadirji.

With the intention of preserving, documenting and digitizing every object entrusted to the AIF and thus giving access to the largest possible number of interested parties, an institutional agreement between the Chadirji Foundation—created by Rifat Chadirji and Balkis Charara Chadirji—and the AIF took the form of a long-term loan. This collection in its breadth and diversity was one of the most complex ever to enter the AIF. At the end of four years of attempts to fundraise for the intended activity, only the catalog of architectural sheets had been partially inventoried, numbered and digitized for the purpose of the exhibition and this publication. This imprint on this system of objects as effected by the archival practices of the AIF, be it in terms of displacement, physical handling, marking or digital recording, engendered new attributes. These acts charged the objects and their systems with new meanings, to bring out a multiplicity of articulations.[4] These acts invite new interpretations, through different formats and discourses with multiple and unlimited narrative structures.

Every Building in Baghdad[5] was an actuation of part of the collection, a curated exhibition, a communicative action that responded to the intention of disseminating the ethnographic and urban photography and architectural documentation produced by Chadirji. While it emerges with a specific theoretical formulation, the exhibition's mobility and circulation allow for an exchangeable, diverse and porous understanding of the archive, and trigger new actions.

In 2016, the *0294ch* collection became an uninhabited container. It was emptied of its physical contents which, in accordance with the wishes the will of Rifat Chadirji, were transferred to the Agha Khan Documentation Center at MIT (AKDC@MIT), to be reunited with the rest of his archive.

The physical contents were 68 binders, color-coded—red, blue, green, yellow and black—gathering photographic documentation classified by date of production, geographical area or theme (rural scenery, fishing, bridges, cooking, music, dance, portraiture, social life, skills, cemeteries, feasts), to which 34 gray binders were added, forming the famous index of architectural sheets.

All of these binders, along with one leather and five plastic folders, left Beirut to become *The Kamil and Rifat Chadirji Photographic Archive* at AKDC@MIT, to become other, elsewhere, and open to new activations.

Today, the Agha Khan Documentation Center is digitizing the collection. The Center agreed to share its work with the foundation. Soon, the *0294ch* collection will be filled again with the digital surrogates. The propagation of the now digital collection independently from its archival source falls into the continuum aspect of the dynamics of this particular archive.

The starting point for this publication is the end point of the Chadirji collection's physical existence at the AIF. It constitutes a mediation, offering an escape from the dichotomy between the material presence of the objects produced and the volatility of the traces of memory registered by Chadirji.

It brings together a selection of 200 sheets, an orderly choice, presented by Mark Wasiuta and Akram Zaatari. At once a narrative, a visual system, an index, a resource and an object of desire, this publication stigmatizes this archive with its hidden dynamics, confronts it with its own unresolved questions, and binds it to the desires of its maker.

1 Elizabeth Edwards, "Photographs: Material Form and the Dynamic Archive", in Caraffa, Costanza. (ed.) *Photo archives and the photographic memory of art history.* Berlin, Deutscher Kunstverlag, 2011, 47.

2 Elizabeth Edwards, *ibidem*, 51.

3 Eric Ketelaar, "Tacit Narratives: The Meanings of Archives", *Archival Science 1* (2001), 138. Ketelaar proposes calling the semantic genealogy of the archive its characteristic to be a "repository of meaning", the multilayered, multifaceted meanings hidden in archiving, which can be deconstructed and reconstructed, then interpreted over and over again.

4 The archive understood in its wider sense, "defines a particular level: that of a practice that causes a multiplicity of statements to emerge", Michel Foucault, *The Archeology of Knowledge*, trans. A. M. Sheridan Smith, Vintage Books, New York, 2010.

5 *Every Building in Baghdad: The Rifat Chadirji Archives at the Arab Image Foundation* is an exhibition that originated at the Arthur Ross Architecture Gallery at Columbia University's Graduate School of Architecture, Planning and Preservation and was curated by Mark Wasiuta, Adam Bandler, and Florencia Alvarez. The exhibition was presented later at the Graham Foundation, Chicago and LAXART, Los Angeles.

Cybernetic Archival Interaction

Mark Wasiuta

IRQ/315/186

Paper is multimedia. So is the building. The archive is multiple. For example, IRQ/315/186. 1970–1975. Central Post, Telephone & Telegraph Offices: nine sheets; thirty photographs. Some black and white, some color. One a photocopy of a 35 mm slide. We see the building from across the Tigris. We see it in construction, then completed. We see its striated but otherwise blank rear face. We see an improbable floating arcade with arches, ribs, and vaults stretched to the top of the tower. Sometimes the building appears in isolation and at other times deep within the city. One view shows it hovering behind Baghdad's double-decker buses—a detail that recalls the British Protectorate and Iraq's UK inheritance. It cuts diagonally, then it is upright and inert. As camera views shift, the building recedes, approaches, lifts, drops, and stutters across the page.

In these sheets we follow the photographic and perceptual adjustments for an object seen, seen again, seen in repetition, and seen comparatively. These multiplying views are one sort of multimedia machine, never stopping or settling into a single frame. In the photos, above the building sits a cluster of satellite dishes, antennae, and shortwave receivers. The page, the photos, the building, the historical markers, are all transmitting. While the sheets are active visually, they are also activated by different stages and forms of production, representation, and communication.

That we are looking at photographs is entirely evident. Equally clear is that we are also viewing a sequence of sheets inscribed with codes, titles, dates, and numbers—sometimes typed, sometimes scrawled. We are looking at photographs filed by a system of schematization and annotation, ordered by multiple reference numbers and codes. We are also looking at photography *as* system of organization and historical notation that aligns archive, architecture, and city.

If the archive and its filing systems became the "dominant institutional basis for photographic meaning" in the early 20th century, these sheets speak fluently that historical dialect, as clerical objects aggressively flaunting their administrative format.[1] They constitute the document foundation of an archive, but one that reveals the twists and folds of archival authority and legibility, one that cedes part of its schematization to the obscured, the deleted, and the erased. It is an archive that speaks an authorial idiolect as much as it does a bureaucratic Esperanto.

Every Building in Baghdad

We first encountered these sheets and their enigmatic code when in Beirut to study collecting institutions in the Levant and Gulf States.[2] Visiting the Arab Image Foundation (AIF) we were struck by its curious double identity, appearing as an institution purposefully and strategically unbalanced. Committed to collecting and preserving the photography of the Arab world—with the technical, scientific expertise this task requires—the AIF is also an artists' project of sorts. Akram Zaatari, along with a group of other local artists, formed the AIF following the Lebanese Civil War, recognizing the cultural, political, and historical importance of assembling its records, with their complicated facticity and indexicality. The AIF treats its collection and archives as a source from which artists and other researchers will not merely clarify, identify, and solidify interpretation, but will also compose new works that challenge the histories, identities, and images of the Arab world. The AIF devotes itself to the labor of securing and stabilizing its collection of photographs, and to the work of unsettling and dislodging histories through alternative readings of images and their claims to archival authority.

The sheets collected in this book were assembled by Iraqi architect Rifat Chadirji. Through the work of his architectural office, Iraq Consult, and in his other roles, Chadirji was a pivotal cultural figure in Baghdad during its postwar modernization. As an architect, a planning consultant, and director of buildings for several government agencies, Chadirji was central to the organization and consolidation of the image of the postwar city. He was also an obsessive photographer. The sheets compiled here include some of the nearly 100,000 photographs Chadirji shot of his buildings and of Baghdad and its surrounding region from the 1950s to the 1970s. The sheets, their content, their system of architectural and photographic coding, a selection of his other photographs, and their multiple, migratory, and mixed archival media status were the basis of our exhibition *Every Building in Baghdad: the Rifat Chadirji Archives at the Arab Image Foundation*.[3]

In communication with the agenda of the AIF, the exhibition opened a view into Chadirji's building, photography, and archival work to speak about other Modernisms and the fate of cities, architecture, and culture in conflict zones. It also pursued questions about collecting systems, archives, and the status of documents—their evidentiary, rhetorical, aesthetic, and informational features. In this sense the exhibition maintained a split focus. It centered on Chadirji, but not his biography or his impressively large body of built work. Rather it considered the archival context through which we came to know

1 Alan Sekula, "The Body and the Archive," *October* 39 (1986): 56. Sekula is commenting on the ordering of images in the police filing cabinets of Alphonse Bertillon in Paris. He is also alluding to the growing reliance on photography within other empirical disciplines from "art history to military intelligence" and to the emerging bibliographic protocols for arranging and correlating photographs— the structural origin of a vast image archiving enterprise at the turn of the last century. Chadirji's sheets are not only governed by such an archival filing logic, they anticipate and prepare for it. Each is a photo-record: image and inscription, photographic and bibliographic entry.

2 The enigma is related to the sheets' precise archival logic and their seeming inconsistencies. We know the sheets use a tripartite code and that the first component locates the project by country. But there are competing explanations and interpretations for the rest. We believe that the second element indexes building type— such as office, residence, or factory—based on the SFB (Samarbetskommitten for Byggnadsfragor) classification system developed in Sweden in the 1950s and adapted for use in the UK in the early 1960s. However, Chadirji's sheets appear to be variably encoded. They sometimes use a two-digit building classification and sometimes three. The third element is a serial number Chadirj assigned to each of his projects. While there is a discernible chronological pattern to the serial number sequence it is also inconsistent.

3 The exhibition was first produced and shown at the Arthur Ross Architecture Gallery at Columbia University's Graduate School of Architecture, Planning, and Preservation in 2016. I researched and curated the exhibition with Florencia Alvarez and Adam Bandler. It has since been shown at the Graham Foundation in Chicago (2016) and LAXART in Los Angeles (2018).

Chadirji and the formation, circulation, and preservation of his documents.

Vulnerable Archives

We know how to think about the authority of the archive, but not about its vulnerability. During our first visit to the AIF we were astonished by director Zeina Arida's description of the challenges of safeguarding the archives in a city with few state-supported institutions and many types of instability.[4] We were shown the archival core of the AIF, the climate-controlled photo vault that secures the collection from environmental degradation. We learned that while saving the photographic legacy of the Arab world from disappearance, collecting introduces its own frailties and dangers. Perhaps in jest—maybe mocking our gullibility—or to underscore the challenges faced by the AIF, Zeina noted that she hoped to raise money for blast walls and other such protections. In her narrative, emergency planning involves both managing systemic power interruptions and guarding against potential strikes, explosions, and debris. The precariousness of Beirut is a perpetual operational concern in which the conventional atmospheric protections of the museum meet military fortifications, whether in fact or in a defensive archival imaginary.

The archival imaginary of the AIF and Chadirji's documents converge around similar issues of vulnerability, threat, and insecurity. At the AIF the objects of preservation are the image content of photographs, their chemical stability, as well as the marks and defects of their history.[5] For the AIF and for Chadirji's archives, the documents act as a material registration of the forces that form them and that compel their circulation.

As a theorist and author of more than ten books on architecture and on the difficulties faced by architects in the Middle East, Chadirji has been critical both of a naïve engagement with local building craft and of the importation of a bland international mode of construction. He characterizes the dominant approach to building in Iraq from the 1950s to the early 1980s as indifferent to the particular social and technical demands of the region and as a "labyrinth of social prejudices, unrealistic fantasies, imported technologies and defective, half-digested or misinterpreted imported symbols and fashions."[6]

Over the decades of his practice, Chadirji tried to reconcile advanced building techniques with architectural antecedents drawn from Iraq's long history. His historical orientation responded to the unbridgeable gap he saw between the technical and social capacities of Iraq and the destabilizing imposition of an internationalism tied to the burgeoning postwar oil economy. The wealth oil generated, outside financial interest, internal political reactions and coups, inappropriate building technologies, culturally homogenizing pan-Arabism, and ill-informed Western projections of Arab identity, were all wrapped into his conception of internationalism. The city and its buildings were the product of this internationalism and its instabilities—whether compliant, reactive, or resistant.

Preoccupied by the transformative effects of these pressures, Chadirji undertook regular photographic expeditions into the streets of Baghdad, to its outskirts, and to northern Iraq. He compiled an expansive photograph collection of sites, customs, and conditions he believed were most imperiled. Chadirji's documentation of his buildings was equally haunted by the specter of disruption. He anticipated that—along with Iraq's historical monuments—his own buildings would eventually be under threat, a moment of grim clairvoyance that accurately forecasted the damage suffered during the 2003 Gulf War.[7]

Chadirji's sheets were documentary insurance against his buildings' eventual destruction and disappearance. From one point of view, the organizational matrix of these sheets is the systematic coding and reconstruction of Chadirji's vast building enterprise, fixing and stabilizing architecture within a set of chronological, programmatic, and geographic coordinates. Yet, from another vantage, the sheet structure, its clerical enumeration, and its administrative aesthetic are the registration and inscriptional materialization of an archival, architectural, and historical instability.

In the late 1970s, Chadirji was first imprisoned in Abu Ghraib, then released by Saddam Hussein to supervise the reconstruction and urban planning of Baghdad in preparation for the summit of non-aligned nations.[8] After bearing witness to an accelerated urban renewal project, its decimation of buildings and neighborhoods, and Baghdad's "cement mixer ambience" of the early 1980s, Chadirji fled Iraq for the USA and Harvard University, smuggling with him the negatives from which the photographs on these sheets were eventually printed.[9] The sheets were ordered and composed after Chadirji subsequently moved to London.

The sheets, then, have numerous identities: they are part of an informational system describing every building within Chadirji's architectural oeuvre, they are a device to preserve a complex image of Iraq's experience of modernization, and they are the charged signifiers of the historical and cultural vulnerability that marks his time in Baghdad as well as his departure. They are a retrospective reconstruction project in which a methodical process of ordering and coding merges with a manic and amplified archival impulse. Despite their multiple views and shifting frames the sheets appear, at first, to stabilize and isolate Chadirji's buildings from the urban and political volatility of their context. Yet, as they begin to accumulate, page after page, they reveal the scope of Chadirji's and Iraq's building project. They hint at the conflicted consequences of this scale of construction. It is a lot of building. Whatever the theorization of architectural form, we sense the oil economy and its instabilities—by which Chadirji was so alarmed—pooling around the buildings and in the streets of Baghdad.

4 Zeina Arida was director of the AIF from 1997 to 2014. Currently the AIF is co-directed by Clémence Cottard and Marc Mouarkech. The visit referenced here took place in 2013 during a research trip for a project titled Collecting Architecture Territories. Adam Bandler, Craig Buckley, Jordan Carver, and I traveled with graduate students from Columbia University to several museums and collecting institutions in the region. The visit was organized by Nora Akawi, director of Studio-X in Amman. We were helped in Beirut by Roula Salamoun and Samah Hijawi throughout the trip.

5 I refer in particular to a series of photographs and negatives shown to us during a subsequent visit to the AIF. They were found within Beit Beirut, a cultural center and museum in La Maison Jaune, a residence used as a prominent sniper's nest during the civil war. Scratched, warped, and stained by water and debris, at question was how these signs of distress would be preserved. The preservation of photographic collateral damage is evidence of its newly assigned testimonial value.

6 Rifat Chadirji, *Concepts and Influences: Towards a Regionalized International Architecture. (London: KPI, 1986),* 39.

7 Heavily bombed, Chadirji's Central Post, Telephone & Telegraph Offices building was also heavily photographed during the war. Through this second barrage of documentation, Chadirji's archive met another system and logic of collection. The archives multiply. The telephone and telegraph offices entered Getty Images coded as 161957702/ Getty Images/ AFP. Chadirji's anticipatory archive and the later collections of Getty Images as well as various postwar building damage surveys combine as a meta-archival record of Baghdad's different forms of modernization, destruction, and ruination.

8 The summit planned for 1982 was eventually canceled due to the Iran-Iraq war and concern for the safety of delegates. The Seventh Summit of the Non-Aligned Movement was held the following year in New Delhi.

9 Timothy McNulty, "War has Iraq's Hussein Looking West," *Chicago Tribune,* November 28, 1982.

But the underlying volatility is perhaps less attached to Baghdad than it is to the sheets' mobility. First negatives, then prints, and now as the sheets reproduced here, Chadirji's documents have migrated from Baghdad to Cambridge, London, and Beirut, and have crossed the ocean yet again to Cambridge where they are held at MIT. Our study of collecting institutions around the world suggested that those objects that circulate most freely slide along the greased corridors of global capital. Chadirji's documents have a certain value and prominence, to be sure. But the relentless migration of his materials is less a mark of privilege than a signal of the impossibility of their return to Baghdad and of their seemingly perpetual separation from the drawings, plans, and office files that form the complete collection of Chadirji's documents.[10] The migrating archive is a category distinct from the circulating image. The itinerant mobility of his documents and their unfixity is a product of and perpetual reflection on Baghdad, its past, and its recurring destabilization. Their mobility is the flashing sign—the wailing siren—of archival precariousness and vulnerability.

Cybernetic Archival Interaction

The sheets hint at Chadirji's relentless documentation drive, confirmed by the staggering number of negatives and photographs in the collection. But the majority of the images in the archives are not of his buildings and are not on these sheets—they are the tens of thousands of photographs that Chadirji shot of the streets of Baghdad, its outer reaches, and its inhabitants. Similarly governed by an impulse to document, hold, and secure that characterizes the photographs of his own buildings, Chadirji's street photography is guided by his sense of the destructive effects of the internationalism that unsettled Baghdad and Iraq in its postwar period.[11] Still following that impulse to order, preserve, and encode, these photographs are organized by a thematic system that categorizes location, activity, or monument. Headings range from Shopping, to Signs and Advertisements, North Iraq, and Architecture—the latter encompassing ancient monuments, traditional housing structures, and (with surprising regularity) images of buildings mid-demolition along Haifa and Rashid streets, the main axes of Baghdad's urban development in the 1970s and 1980s.

Although the two sets of Chadirji's photographs share a deep preoccupation with the disappearance and destruction of Baghdad and an equally nervous reaction to its modernization, they are not identical twins. Aside from their content and the ethnographic slant of his street photography, they evince different modes of viewing, organizing, and archiving, and make distinct declarations and observations about the temporality of destruction. Chadirji's building enterprise and its photography—and their attempt to absorb and redirect international pressures and influences—contain the threat of Iraq's political instabilities and financial insecurities within the language of historical and technical reconciliation. The visual repetition of the building sheets and the hallucinatory surface agitation of projects like the National Insurance Company—IRQ/320/151—vibrate with the force of internationalism and the enfolding energy of Chadirji's regional sublimations. Yet, for his buildings, Chadirji deferred the prospect of degradation and damage to the future.

In contrast, his street photography confronts the destructive effects of Baghdad's modernization more directly and immediately. His photographs track the bulldozers and backhoes, their trail of rubble, and the clouds of building dust that settle on the city in the 1970s. He also searches the streets for the social life and spaces of social interaction that will soon be displaced and dismantled. His forays into the city compelled a shift in photographic method. Especially during the last decade of Chadirji's time in Iraq, the figure of the man on the street with a camera—assumed to be an agent of state surveillance—was viewed with suspicion and hostility. One result is that the informality and speed of Chadirji's street photographs became exaggerated. Unlike his studied building portraiture, these photographs are not well-composed tableaux so much as covert attempts to capture images of vulnerable locations and populations.

Chadirji's path was likely less an aimless documentary *dérive* than a geographic survey informed by insider urban trading. As the most prominent architect and planner in Baghdad, Chadirji was all too aware of the pattern of erupting demolitions. Referencing this pattern, the archival logic of his street photography imposes an order onto the images and the city both. Baghdad is archived across a taxonomy of spatial and social disruption tied to the geographic distribution of modernization. With social scenes and behaviors indexed by location, the archive maps the city by proximity to zones of demolition and active modernization or to sites not yet modernized. The structural numerical code on Chadirji's building sheets organizes his work by building type and program. The new appearance of cinemas, factories, office buildings, and telecommunications headquarters and the disorder of urban transformation they represent appear stabilized in the archives through a coherent process of typologically directed modernization—the sheets replace social upheaval with a categorically, chronologically, determined structure of knowledge. Similarly, in the street photography archive the city mutates into a matrix of distributed and tagged customs, traditions, and social behaviors.

The two photo sets reveal Chadirji straddling two modes of work: his architectural practice, which he argues is an act against the destabilization of a perfidious internationalism, and his photography of the city, which— like the documentation of his buildings—is an act of visual preservation. They are governed by a similar but unequal lament. The first is an approach to building that attempts to guide Iraq's modernization. The second articulates and catalogues loss—not through the violence and conflict to come but through the violence of modernization in which he was also an agent, willing or not.

Like the photos in his building sheets Chadirji's city photographs are cheap, unstable prints. They are shot in black and white but have started to shift toward purple and brown tones—as though chemically striving for a hint of the chromatic vibrancy that appears in his building photography but sacrificed here to a journalistic aesthetic. At the edges of his building photographs, we sometimes see people, cars, buses, and other details that invade the shots, pull the architecture out of its isolation and back into the social and political economy of the city. These urban elements and actors seem to jump across one photo archive to the other, shuttling between two distinct representational and discursive spaces. Like the satellite dishes and antennae on the Central Post, Telephone & Telegraph Offices, they suggest a transmission between the two forms of work. And while this relay seems natural—both sets are Chadirji's photographs after all—these signals are also a perturbation, an interference between two starkly different archival and architectural positions.

10 In their current location at MIT's Aga Khan Documentation Center, Chadirji's photographs and sheets have been reunited with drawings and other materials from his Baghdad office, marking an end to the hope that the full archive would eventually return to Baghdad.

11 Rifat Chadirji described these and other motivations for his extensive photography project during an interview in London that took place in November 2015.

In the first position, architecture is a formal, technical, typological, and linguistic system. In the second, architecture is entangled in the politics, economies, and social texture of the city, with its multiple environments and ecologies. As the communication line between Chadirji's two sets of photographs shows, these positions can never be fully autonomous—their independence erodes almost as soon as it is declared. In Chadirji's archive the tension between these two poles is almost physically and spatially legible, as though Chadirji, with his camera, is perpetually pivoting to look at architecture as categorical object and then the city as social interaction, oscillating between these modes and objects of observation. This relay underscores that Chadirji's archive is not the photos or the prints, but this representational dyad and its tensions. Beyond its material documents and their inscriptions, the archive is this structure that provides and shapes the terms of discourse. The archive is architectural photography's discursive spaces.

One of Chadirji's most unusual theoretical devices is "cybernetic interaction." Although he concedes that by the 1970s computation offered the possibility of a fluid process of input, response, and adaptation, he is primarily referring to an early period of "manu-aesthetic" production in which building techniques evolved in harmony with material properties.[12] Cybernetic archival interaction would describe how the two sets of photographs develop within a series of exchanges implicit to the discursive properties of the archive. Through this interaction, these archives, the archive, is not only multiple, but also organized through these distinct modes of chronicling and their structural interdependence. The instability of these sheets is not only a result of their mobility, or visual agitation, it emanates from the interfering, interruptive logics of these two forms of photographic observation and their declarations about Baghdad, its building, its oil economy, its politics, and its devastation to come.

12 Chadirji, 30.

THE FOLD

Akram Zaatari

"… A story inhabits the memory of each one of us, inhabits the features, the face and the words with which we speak."

Rifat Chadirji[1]

The fold is the pleat formed by turning or bending a part of a material such as fabric, paper or even sedimentary rock or soil. The fold is the form the material takes after such an event. It is also the trace that is left on the material, the crease that marks the location of turning or pressing.

Inherent in folding is that material turns, hence occupies or engages with the space around it. Folding is a basic step in creating a three-dimensional form. A ribbon becomes a flower. A sheet of paper becomes a box. The fold turns material in such a way as to cover parts with other parts, changing its original form.

When the fold is accidental or natural, as with aging matter or in geological shifts, or in reaction to climatic conditions, the material undergoes a permanent deformation, the end form of which is unpredictable. When a fold is intentional, it reorganizes material to create a new form, increase or reduce volume, confine or rearrange space to create storage or organize access, for example.

When intentional, the fold is a creative action involving pre-scripted steps and sometimes requiring a considerable level of precision, like folding a sheet of paper into an origami, or several sheets to make a book.

The fold is a form of narration.

Folding is a selective process. It sacrifices parts for a purpose. It conceals some parts and highlights others, like folding clothes to store them on a shelf or fit them into a container of specific dimensions. It is like folding a sheet of paper into an airplane, so that it can travel through the air. The fold is a kind of edit.

Folding is the simplest way to enclose space, to conceive of space within folds. The fold is an edge. It both demarcates and structures space. Folding is the simplest way to form a structure.

Unfolding is undoing, deconstructing, dismantling, turning material back into its original form. The creases in an unfolded material contain its history and, in a way, save it from amnesia. The history of material inscribes itself in creases. When unfolded, material testifies that history has already found its way into it, through the fold. "To unfold" is not the opposite of "to fold," but an extension of it, essential in identifying it, analyzing it or revealing its structure. Deleuze writes:

> The unfold: certainly not the opposite of the fold, nor its effacement, but the continuation or the extension of its act, the condition of its manifestation. When the fold ceases to be represented and becomes a "method," an operation, an act, the unfold becomes the result of the act which is expressed in precisely that way.[2]

The fold or pleat, as the result of a fold and unfold, is the memory of material.

Within archival practice, the fold's primary function is to contain and provide efficient access, when needed. The "folder" is a container of disparate folded items brought together for a reason, like a tag they may share, a size, a time period. The "folder" is a by-product of an archival practice, which is, in itself, a branch of library science. A folder has both a structural function in a larger archive, and a narrative one as a binder of contents. It organizes items within its folds thematically, alphabetically or temporally, for example. But a folder also preserves the separate identity of each item within it and preserves the possibility of reorganizing items over and over within the same folder or migrating them to different folders to follow a different order. A catalog enumerates items and arranges them following a system of classification. The catalog organizes items such that they may function best within a specific practice. A sales catalog, for example, provides a community of buyers with details of all items offered for sale so they can select an item to buy. Within a professional creative practice such as design, a catalog is an index of previous works, like a portfolio of all works produced by an author, a company, a designer or artist. It features samples of their work and gives an insight into their characteristics. It displays the work's qualities and demonstrates its potential.

1 Chadirji's own words describing his prison mates in Abu Ghraib prison in Baghdad.
From: Chadirji, R. and Charara, B. *Jidar Bayna Zulmatayn*, (*A Wall Between One Darkness and Another*), Beirut, Dar Al Saqi, 2003.

2 Deleuze, Gilles and Strauss, Jonathan, "The Fold," p. 243 *Yale French Studies*, no. 80, Yale, 1991, pp. 227–47.

The Photograph

Every photograph is an exposure of a view of something or somewhere. Just as folding confines space, a photograph captures it and folds it into a flat image, offsetting parts of a scene against others, covering parts entirely with others. Every photograph hides parts of a scene to reveal others. Every photograph reproduces in miniature what is much bigger in life and brings somewhere an image of somewhere else somewhere distant and out of sight. The impact of a fold in a photographed space is permanent, in the sense that hidden or obscured parts in a picture are irretrievable. What a photograph missed that was present at the time of exposure—due to the camera's point of view or exposure or any limitation in the technology used—will remain inaccessible.

In the folds within a photograph lies a history; lie many histories. A single photograph is not enough to seize the totality of a situation or a space as an example. Architects take multiple photographs to document a space, a construction, a building site. They record different elevations, angles, interiors, and details. Each photograph represents an aspect of a space, a facet of a place or building. The more photographs produced, the more details recorded. The more diverse the angles from which photographs are taken, the better three-dimensional space is described, as in photogrammetry. The ultimate documentation aims to leave no room for the fold, as in seamless 360° interactive photographs.

The fold in a photograph is a detail that triggers a process. Through it a different narrative—from that of the photograph itself—unfolds. It is a feature through which the initial construction of a photograph—its making—is undone. It bears the history of a photograph, its memory, and that may allow its unfolding. If the purpose of a picture is to narrate or describe space, it is fair to say that the folds in it may tell the story of the maker's practice, for example, or the limitations of the medium used.

The Contact Sheet

A contact sheet is an entire numbered sequence that lists visually all the photographs taken by the photographer in a given space or location, during a specific work session, or those exposed on a given roll of film. A contact sheet is to a single photograph, what a folder is to an item within it.

A contact sheet is indifferent to the quality of each photograph. It displays the entire sequence, including those shots that might have failed or which the photographer doubted and repeated. It is a log sheet made with icons that serves only the photographer and, presumably, is not made to be exhibited. It is meant to be a reference for the maker within a practice. It serves as a basis for evaluating work and making a selection.

The fold in time is the representation of time shortened, as in literature, illustration, comics, and, typically, in film. The fold in time is the ellipsis. It manifests itself in the cut. The fold within a narrative is what the viewer perceives as the jump in time that acknowledges the existence of a time that is hidden. When perceived through the timeframe of the film, the ellipsis hints at missing narratives outside the film time. In a film, the cut is language, as is the fold. A photographic contact sheet enfolds time between frames; looking at a contact sheet allows the viewer to identify the time lapses between frames. It is possible to identify a photographer's effort to seize additional information in a certain scene, take a better picture, change position, or reframe, etc. A photographer's work is not restricted to the time of the click, otherwise the life of a great photographer at work, as William Klein cynically underlined, would add up to no more than minutes at most, given that each photograph takes 1/125 of a second to expose. Photography, as a practice, takes place in-between frames, in hidden time, either before or after a photograph is taken. The work of the photographer, therefore, is hidden in the contact sheet, as the work of the archivist is hidden in the folds of the catalog.

In March 2012, the Iraqi architect Rifat Chadirji deposited his photographic archive at the Arab Image Foundation hoping to digitize and gradually annotate it. The archive was transported from a Lebanese customs depot directly to Chadirji's villa in Halat, north of Beirut. When the archivist arrived at the location, the material was in some disorder, but three parts could still be identified. The first was the photographic work of Kamil Chadirji, Rifat's father, a significant figure in Iraq's political and social history. The second was the photographic documentation of Rifat's architecture projects, including sheets dedicated to each one. Although the sheets were loosely folded, they were carefully numbered and marked-up. They looked as if they were made to produce a catalogue raisonné of Rifat's architecture. The third was Rifat's own photographic work, consisting of prints organized thematically in albums depicting various aspects of life in Iraq. For him, they are like reflections on a changing place and people going through major urban and societal shifts.[3]

Chadirji's architecture sheets are intriguing. They were produced at the peripheries of three overlapping practices not far removed from folding: architecture, photography, and library science. They consist of white A4 sheets documenting Chadirji's architecture projects photographically. From time to time, they include photographic reproductions of drawings or models, but in most cases, they present photographs of built projects in Iraq and other Arab states.[4]

Each project is given an alphanumeric reference, typed or inscribed by hand on the top edge of every sheet. Photographs are glued onto the sheet with numbers inscribed by hand at the bottom of each picture, sometimes to the right and sometimes to the left. In most cases, they are given the same numbers as the edge numbers on the negatives they were printed from. Some sheets have two punch marks in their left margins, indicating they have been part of a binder, but most remain unpunched.

The photographs on the sheets vary in size and format. They are organized following a varying grid structure. Some photographs have been cut out of contact sheets and pasted onto a blank sheet of paper; others have been enlarged in different sizes to show details. Sometimes a photographic easel is used as a cache while printing and therefore images have a thin pure white border around them, whereas in other instances frames were enlarged with a black border that represents the transparent film around the image on a given negative.[5]

3 Many of those reflections were recorded in an audio interview with Chadirji, made by Ralph Nashawati (AIF) for archiving purposes in March and August 2012.
4 This publication includes the sheets that list projects in the Gulf region, mainly in Iraq, and in Abu Dhabi, Bahrain, and Kuwait.
5 In contact prints, images appear as icons printed at the same size of the negative on black sheet. When the border around an image is white, it means that the printer used an easel to crop out the black, maintaining the white background of sensitized printing paper as a white frame. Surprisingly, many of the photographs of projects are reproduced the same size as the negative, sometimes 56 × 56 mm (in the case of 120 rolls exposed with a 6 × 6 camera) or 24 × 36 mm (in the case of 135 rolls), and yet icons have white borders around the image.

On some sheets, a part of a contact sheet with many strips is pasted onto the A4 sheet without cutting the images, preserving the negative's edge numbers and perforations. It looks like a shortcut decision that was taken to save time. In other cases, negative strips are slightly enlarged as a whole, with multiple frames in them, including perforations and edge numbers. But to highlight those numbers, sometimes original numbers are covered with patches of white correction fluid on which the same numbers have been re-inscribed with a black marker.

Occasionally, annotations on the sheet indicate that the photographs on it were printed from color slides, or sometimes even as black and white reproductions of color slides. Chadirji was concerned with the quality of prints mounted on the sheets, even when he did not have the time or the possibility of making proper prints. He addresses the issue in a note on sheet IRQ/812/312, saying: "All these color prints are cheap direct prints from slides. Can get better-quality prints."

Upon their arrival at the AIF, the sheets were placed in gelatin sleeves, often paired with the negatives that contain the images. Several sheets are dedicated to each project, totaling just under 300, of which 201 are included in this book. Some of them appear to have been produced with more care than others, depending on the person doing the job and the time allocated to the work. Some annotations are scrawled but have been typed out or rewritten neatly at the top of the sheet. Notes written in Arabic in a sketchy manner, such as clients' names, for example, are also retranscribed properly in English at the top of the sheets. It looks as if Chadirji has been through them and identified projects, pointed out mistakes, and returned the sheets to an assistant. There is an interesting staggering of times in those documents. It is obvious that the production across the three practices—architecture, photography and cataloguing—did not happen in parallel. Some projects were documented while under way, others only once completed and sometimes much later, when time permitted. It seems that Chadirji himself documented his projects when he had the time.

Furthermore, selecting and organizing photographs and linking them to projects while creating sheets for each one does not seem to have happened at the same time as the photographic documentation, but at a later stage. Chadirji confirmed that the catalog was made in London in the 1990s, more than ten years after he left Iraq and stopped practicing architecture.

It also looks as if groups of sheets were produced together at certain times, and other groups at other times. For example, a large number of sheets are made with a pre-printed A4 template. It is a sheet divided longitudinally, in the form of a contact sheet, into four rows to accommodate four strips of 35 mm film. Each row has a two-digit-number printed beneath it to the left, the first referring to the number of the strip and the second referring to first picture in the row. They start with 11, 21, 31, and 41. Other sheets start with 51, 61, 71 and 81, assuming that two sheets could cover a single project. It seems as if the person who made the sheets and catalog realized that those numbers could be confusing, so all the preprinted numbers on the sheets have been corrected by hand. Typical sheets have seven or eight images, using two rows instead of four and leaving some blank space on the page to breathe. Numbers to the left of every line are always barred or covered by a picture, naturally given a different number. Many sheets use regular blank paper. They are divided so as to fit six, twelve, or eighteen photographs, using the page vertically in most cases.

The Tag

The tag is a part attached to a whole for the purpose of identifying it or something in it. The tag can be a visual or textual mark, or a hint enabling an item to be associated with a group of other items sharing the same tag. In library science, the most common tag is the keyword. Visually, it may translate into a mark like a symbol or a color.

On the sleeves that house Chadirji's architecture sheets, many circular color tags point at specific areas. They sometimes point at frames. Do they flag those selected to be enlarged, as is typical with contact sheets? Do they depict a selection for a publication, or a second reproduction for a client, or maybe hint at other transactions? This is how a catalog is used within a practice.

The circumstances in which Chadirji packed his belongings—including his negatives—left Baghdad, and gradually closed his office in the 1980s, dedicating himself from then on to theory, writing, teaching, and cataloguing his former architectural practice, must have been reflected in his photographs. From then on, they served as a catalog of a discontinued practice and illustrated his writing. Chadirji was to fold and unfold his architectural practice, contrary to extending it. Those same circumstances must have had an impact on his built projects across the Gulf region as well. As opposed to celebrating an architect's practice, enhancing it and providing it with context, from then on, they would testify to its sudden halt. Rather than celebrating the Iraqi modernity they were born into, they testify to its abortion or sickness, and announce themselves as its ruins. For the outsider, aware that these architecture sheets were produced in exile after the permanent suspension of a practice, these tags can only point at a desire that hides in the fold. And because some of the sheets might have been misplaced from their sleeves before reaching the AIF in Beirut and might have occupied other sleeves with tags intended to refer to other photographs on other sheets, sometimes these color tags point at a blank space and sometimes fall halfway between pictures. Most often they point at predictable good exposures with a red, green, or yellow tag. But when the sleeve clearly does not belong to the sheet it enfolds, the tags on it reflect a desire that has been lost in the fold.

In December 2016, Rifat Chadirji donated his entire archive to the Agha Khan Documentation Center at MIT. In January 2017, the last volume of sheets, folders, and photo albums left the AIF for his home in London, and from there to the USA. This publication is intended to offer a snapshot of the condition of Chadirji's architecture catalog, the sheets' state during their short stay at the Arab Image Foundation in Beirut. While preparing this publication, the process of reproducing these sheets triggered significant questions.

Technical reproduction would tend not to consider the tags on the plastic sleeves for two reasons. The first is because the tags are not part of the original documents but are like annotations marked on the envelopes that contained documents. The second is because, even if sheets were to be reproduced inside transparent sleeves—like documents in their containers, like a picture in its frame—in this case, the cheap sleeves that envelop the sheets would detract from the sharpness of their content. But is it not possible to reproduce the sheets without the sleeves and place the color tags digitally on the reproductions of the sheets? Such an attempt to digitally reconstruct the effect of tags on sheets would mean to create documents that do not exist. And to engage with such an attempt would be to re-invent new documents in the process of their reproduction.

But from the perspective of the fold as the memory of material, to reproduce the sheets without tags—as if certain parts did not attract an architect's attention more than others, as if certain photographs did not reproduce more than others, as if the catalog served a continuing building practice, and as if Chadirji did not leave Iraq and quit that practice two years after his release from prison in 1982—is to deny their history and possibly contradict the reason(s) behind their making. To reproduce the sheets bare, dis-considering the fact that they have been in the custody of a foundation that witnessed the early work of Walid Raad on the Atlas group, the early works of Yto Barrada, and that published the writings of Jalal Toufic, notably on the fate of the referent upon the destruction of tons of Iraqi currency carrying the portrait of Saddam Hussein after the US invasion of Iraq[6]—is to dis-consider the theoretical and visual contexts that laid the ground for an appreciation of an aesthetic of labor in the archive, and subsequently the celebration of this collection at the AIF and its exhibition later by Mark Wasiuta at Columbia University's GSAPP in 2016.

When Chadirji's architecture sheets were deposited at the AIF, multiple desires had already inscribed themselves onto them. From within an understanding of documents that considers the "affect" as a transformative action, to reconstitute tags digitally while reproducing the sheets in a book is to embrace their transformation. To depart from standard reproduction conventions is to seek the larger historical precision, even at the risk of inventing new documents, at the risk of pointing at Chadirji's built projects as ghosts of a practice, and at the risk of turning the regional Arab modernity, celebrated in every picture on every sheet, into the postwar ruin it has turned into following the US-led invasion of Iraq in 2003.

6 Toufic, Jalal: "Saving Face," in *Review of Photographic Memory*, Beirut, the Arab Image Foundation, 2004, pp. 6–14.

(1960/03 Film)

BRIDGE

IRQ/18

03

06

02

05

01

04

IRQ/18

BRIDGE

IRQ/18/

10

11

07

08

09

0294ch/IRQ/18(B)

IRQ/18/182

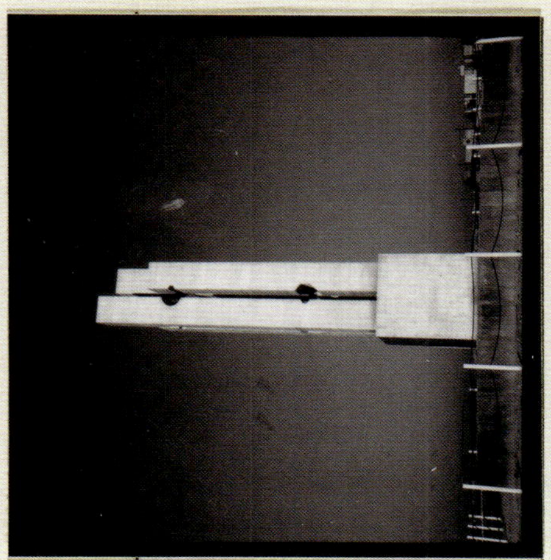

03

06

02

05

01

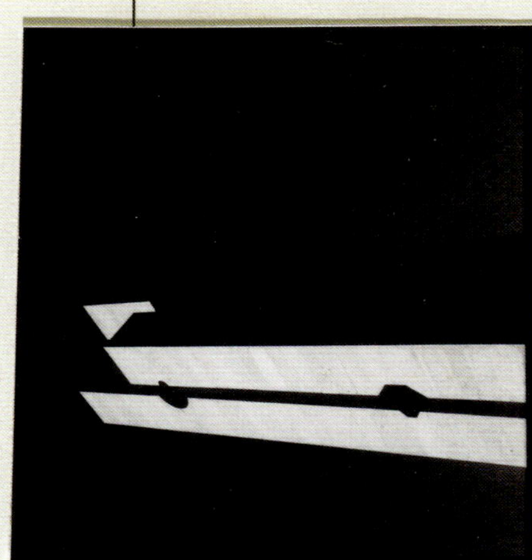

04

IRQ/18/182.

07a

07

71

81

IRQ/18/182 (B)

984/188

IRQ/188/188

0294ch/ARCH/IRQ/984/188 (A)

IRQ/273/169

01

02

03

04

05

06

IRQ/273/189

09

08

07

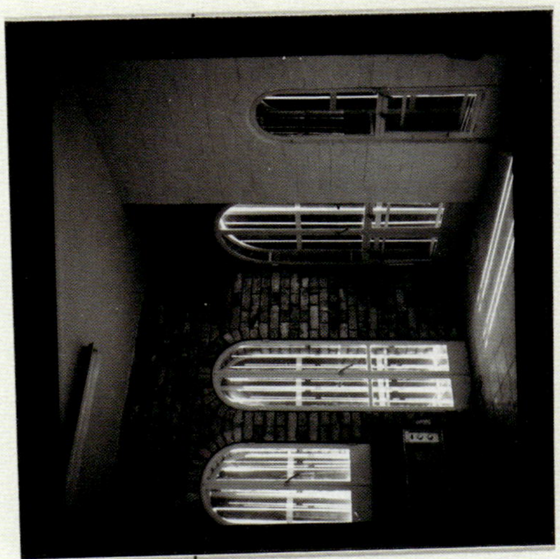

12

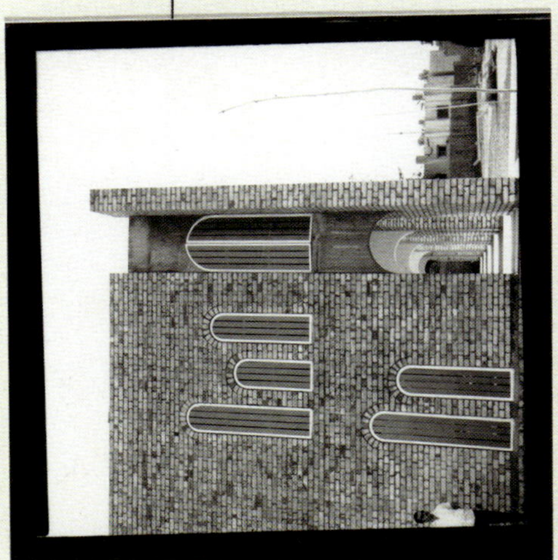

11

10

IRQ/277/159

FLOUR MILL
IRQ/273/161

16

13

17

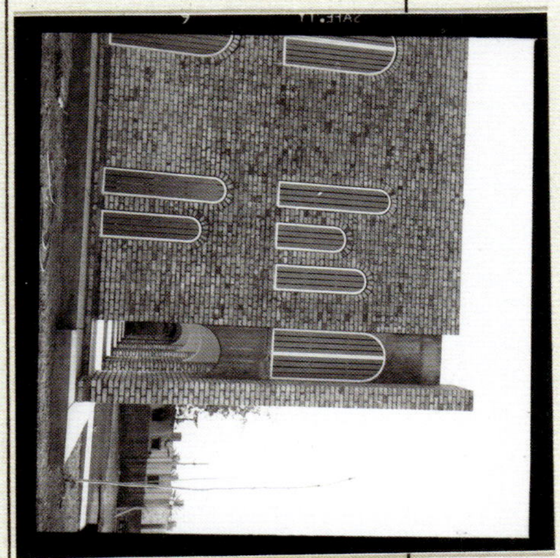

14

18

15

19

20

21

22

23

1970-1971 KUFA CEMENT FACTORY IRQ/277/187

01

02

03

04

05

06

07

08

TOBACCO MONOPOLY - ADMINISTRATION I96I IRQ/3I/IO7

1961
TOBACCO MONOPOLY - ADMIN

IRQ/31/107

01

02

03

04

IRQ/31/107

TOBACCO MONOPOLY . ADMINISTRATION - 1961 IRQ/31/107

TOBACCO MONOPOLY. ADMINISTRATION 1961 IRQ/31/107

10 no neg

09

08

11 no neg

179

INSTITUTE OF MINISTRY OF SOCIAL AFFAIRS, BAGHDAD   IRQ/312

INSTITUTE OF MINISTRY OF SOCIAL AFFAIRS – BAGHDAD

~~IRQ CONSULT OFFICE I.Q.C.~~

179

IRQ/312

01

04

02

05

03

06

INSTITUTE OF MINISTRY OF
~~IRQ CONSULT OFFICE I.Q.C.~~
SOCIAL AFFAIRS - BAGHDAD

314 / 179

IRQ/ 312

07

10

08

11

09

12

314/179

IRQ/312

TRAINING INSTITUTE
MINISTRY OF SOCIAL
AFFAIRS, BAGHDAD

3

4

5

6

7

8

→ 9 → 9A → 10 → 10A

→ 11
→ 11A
→ 12
→ 12A
→ 19
→ 19A
→ 20
→ 20A

COUNCIL OF MINISTERS BUILDING BAGHDAD IRQ/313/302

15

I973 LABOUR TRADE UNION BUILDING IRQ/3I4/223

19

I970-I975 CENTRAL POST, TELEPHONE & TELEGRAPH OFFICES

IRQ/3I5/I86

I970-I975 CENTRAL POST, TELEGRAPH & TELEPHONE OFFICES IRQ/3I5/I86

33A

CENTRAL POST, TELEGRAPH & TELEPHONE OFFICES IRQ/315/186

44.

45.

46.

47.

CENTRAL POST, TELEGRAPH & TELEPHONE OFFICES IRQ/3I5/I86

48.

49.

50.

51.

0294 ch/IRQ/315/186 (G)

52.

53.

54.

55.

1971

CENTRAL POST, TELEGRAPH & TELEPHONE OFFICES IRQ/315/186

56.

57

colour neg.

58

colour neg.

59

colour neg.

60

colour neg.

1971

CENTRAL POST, TELEGRAPH & TELEPHONE OFFICES IRQ/315/186

B+W NEGATIVE FROM COLOUR SLIDE

61

B+W NEG FROM COLOUR SLIDE

62

31

32

33

41

42

43

0294ch/ARCH/IRQ/315/181/ⓔ

I970-I975 CENTRAL POST, TELEGRAPH & TELEPHONE OFFICES IRQ/3I5/I86

36A

→35

→36

→34

~~MUNIR ABBAS BUILDING~~ IRQ/818/9

02

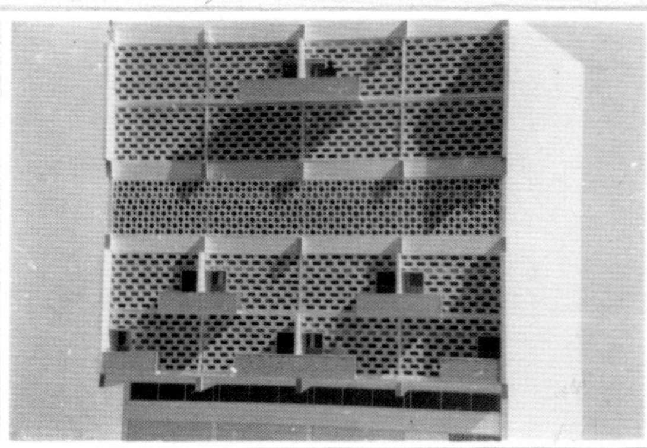

03

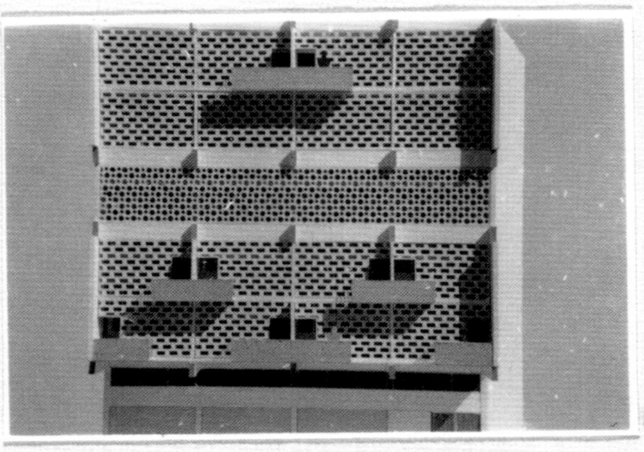

04

05

06

07

Pier Dawood

file 8

320/017

~~MUNIR ABBAS BUILDING~~

IRQ/818/9

08

09

10

11

12

13

14

15

Pir Dawood

~~MUNIR ABBAS BUILDING~~

IRQ/818/9

17

18

19

19

20

21

22

127

IRQ CONSULT OFFICE. I.Q.C. IRQ/32

IRQ/32

01

02

03

0294ch | IRQ | 32 | 127 (G)

IRQ CONSULT OFFICE I.Q.C. 127 IRQ/32

IRQ/32

04

05

06

IRQ CONSULT OFFICE I.Q.C. IRQ/32

127

07

08

IRAQ CONSULT OFFICE IRQ/32

03

02

01

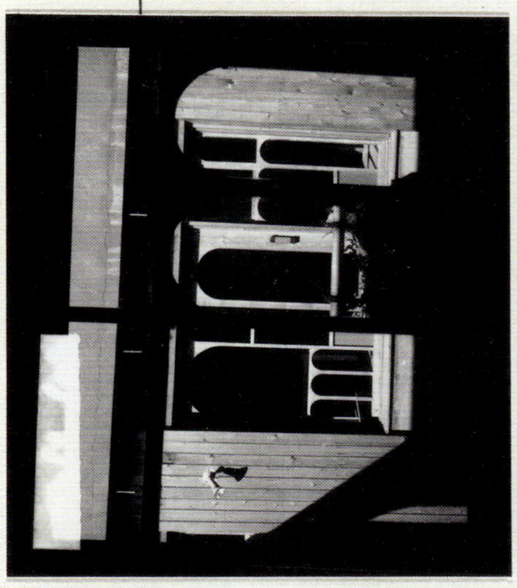

04

05

06

07

05a

08

08a

0294ch/IRQ/32/127 (E)

IRQ/32

09

10

11

12

13

14

0294ch / IRQ / 32 / 127 (F)

IRAQ CONSULT OFFICE

IRQ/32

1969 NATIONAL INSURANCE COMPANY - MOSUL IRQ/320/151

1a

4a

2a

3a

0294ch/IRQ/320/151 (A)

NATIONAL INSURANCE

13

23

12

22

74/48

11

21

31

32

33

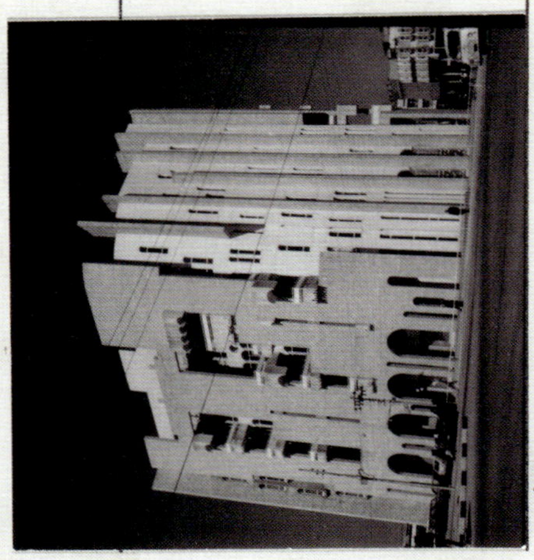
41

42

43

(c)

NATIONAL INSURANCE

13a

23a

12a

22a

74/47

11a

21a

31a

32a

33a

41a

42a

43a

NATIONAL INSURANCE

13 b

12 b

11 b

74/49

0294ch/IRQ/320/151 (F)

33b

43b

32b

42b

31b

41b

FEDERATION OF INDUSTRIES. IRQ/32/153

01

02

03

04

0294ch / IRQ / 32 / 153 (B)

1966 FEDERATION OF INDUSTRIES BUILDING IRQ/32/153

IRQ/32/153-39

0294 ch / IRQ / 32/153 (A)

FEDERATION OF INDUSTRIES IRQ/32/153

35

36

37

38

0294ch/IRQ/32/153(D)

FEDERATION OF INDUSTRIES

IRQ/32/153

13

23

12

22

74/46

11

21

RUHOON BANK IRQ/328/16

01

02

03

04

05

RAFIDAIN BANK - SINAK BRANCH IRQ/328/108

1961

01

02

1970 RAFIDAIN BANK - SALHIYAH BRANCH IRQ/328/165

20

B+W NEG FROM COLOUR SLIDE

COMMERCIAL BANK - MANSOUR IRQ/328/170

IRQ/328/170

01

02

03

04

05

06

IRQ/328/170

09

08

07

10

1970 - COMMERCIAL BANK - MANSOUR IRQ/328/170

B+W NEGATIVES FROM COLOUR SLIDES

20

21

22

331 / 011

HAMED OFFICE BUILDING

IRQ/32

01

02

03

04

05

IRQ/331/013

MUNIR ABBAS BUILDING

IRQ/818/14

01

02

03

04

05

IRQ/331/013

~~MUNIR ABBAS BUILDING~~ الرحى IRQ/818/10

03

04

05

06

07

08

09

10

0294ch/IRQ/331/13(D)

IRQ/331/013

MUNIR ABBAS BUILDING

IRQ/818/13

01

02

03

04

ABBOUD BUILDING

IRQ/3/26

01

02

03

04

05

06

07

08

0294ch/IRQ/331/26 (A)

1969 Waqaf Bldg Almiyah
IRQ/331/195

~~320/195~~

01

1969 WAQAF BUILDING - ALWIYAH IRQ/320/195

1966 TOBACCO MONOPOLY - OFFICES & STORE

IRQ/34/154.

14

1966 TOBACCO MONOPOLY - OFFICES & STORE

IRQ/34/154

~~32~~ 15

~~33~~ 16

~~34~~ 17

1966 TOBACCO MONOPOLY - OFFICE AND STORES IRQ/34/154

NEGATIVES IN COLOUR

18

~~018~~

19

~~02~~

20

~~03~~

1966 TOBACCO MONOPOLY - OFFICE AND STORES IRQ/34/154

~~04~~ 21

~~05~~ 22

A

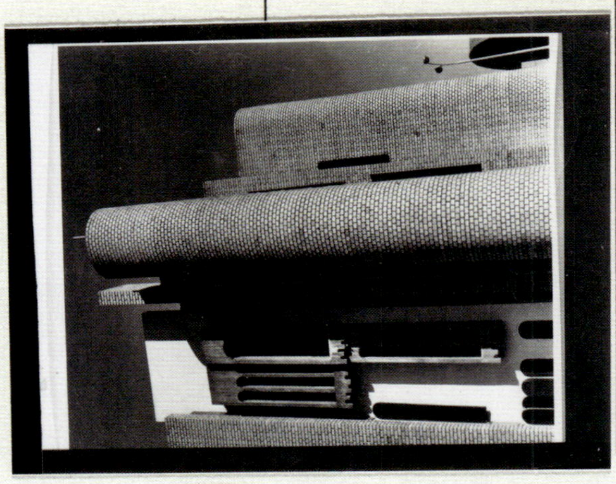

01

02

03

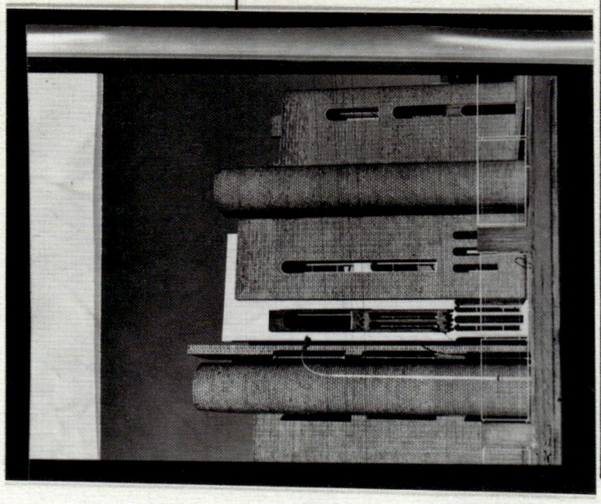

04

05

06

1966 – TOBACCO MONOPOLY IRQ/34/154

B

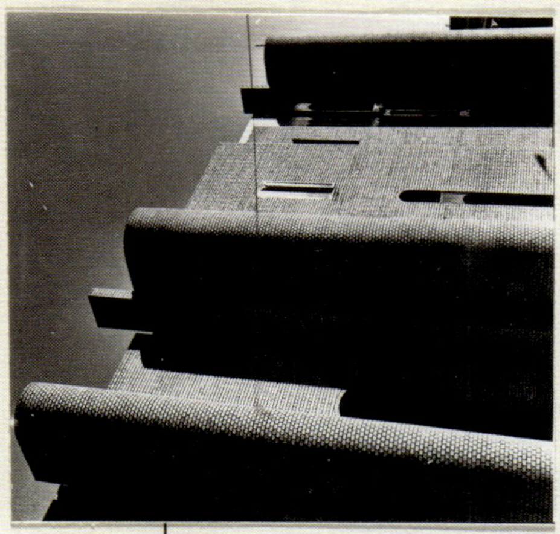

3b

2b

1b

7b

6b

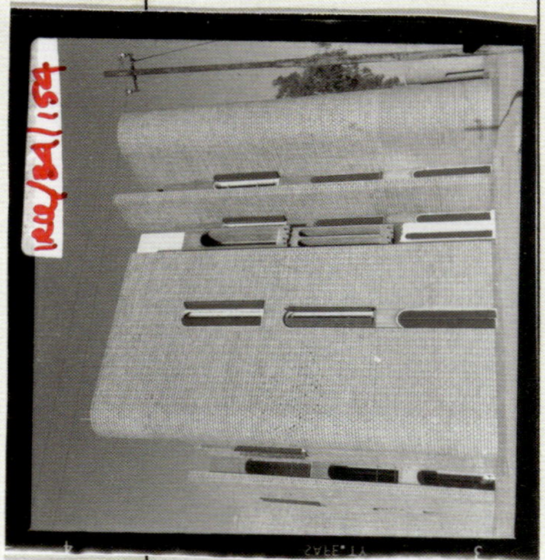

5b

4b

C.

1966 TOBACCO MONOPOLY - OFFICES AND STORES IRQ/34/154

01

02

03

04

05

06

07

08

09

10

11

12

331/066

BUILDING FOR HIDAIB HAMOOD IRQ/342/66

01

02

0294ch/IRQ/331/66 (A)

ARBIL ORPHANAGE IRQ/446/~~166~~

1965. VETERINARY COLLEGE IRQ/72/103 (A)

01

02

03

04

05

06

07

08

09

10

11

11A

0294ch / arch / IRQ / 72 / 103 (A)

1965 - VETERINARY COLLEGE IRQ/72/103 (B)

12

13

14

15

16

17

18

19

20

21

22

23

1965 VETERINARY COLLEGE IRQ/72/103 (C)

31

32

33

34

35

36

37

38

39

40

41

42

0294ch | arch | IRQ | 72 | 103 (C)

1965 VETERINARY COLLEGE IRQ/72/103 (D)

43

44

45

46

47

48

49

50

51

52

53

54

IRAQ SCIENTIFIC ACADEMY I965 IRQ/73I/IO4

001

002

IRAQ SCIENTIFIC ACADEMY 1965 IRAQ/73II04

003

004

IRAQ SCIENTIFIC ACADEMY 1965 IRQ/73I/I04

005

006

IRAQ SCIENTIFIC ACADEMY 1965 IRQ/731/104

007

008

IRAQ SCIENTIFIC ACADEMY I965 IRAQ/73I/IO4

-009

-010

- 011

- 012

0294ch/IRQ/731/104(C)

IRAQ SCIENTIFIC ACADEMY 1965 IRQ/73I/IO4

013

1965 IRAQI SCIENTIFIC ACADEMY IRQ/731/104

20

21

1965 IRAQI SCIENTIFIC ACADEMY IRQ/731/104

22

23

1965 IRAQI SCIENTIFIC ACADEMY IRQ/731/104

24

25

o294ch/arch/IRQ/731/104 (F)

1965 IRAQI SCIENTIFIC ACADEMY IRQ/731/104

26

27

28

1965 IRAQI SCIENTIFIC ACADEMY IRQ/731/104

28

29

30

0294ch / arch / IRQ / 73 / 104 (H)

1965 IRAQI SCIENTIFIC ACADEMY IRQ/731/104

31

32

33

1965 IRAQI SCIENTIFIC ACADEMY IRQ/731/104

44

1967 CHEMICAL LABORATORIES IRQ/732/I88

المجمع العلمي الكردي

10

11

MAATH ALOUSI'S HOUSE

IRQ/812/R

01

02

03

04

05

HUSSAIN JAMIL RESIDENCE, 1955

IRQ/812/3

01

02

03

04

05

HUSSAIN JAMIL RESIDENCE, 1955

IRQ/812/3

06

07

08

09

10

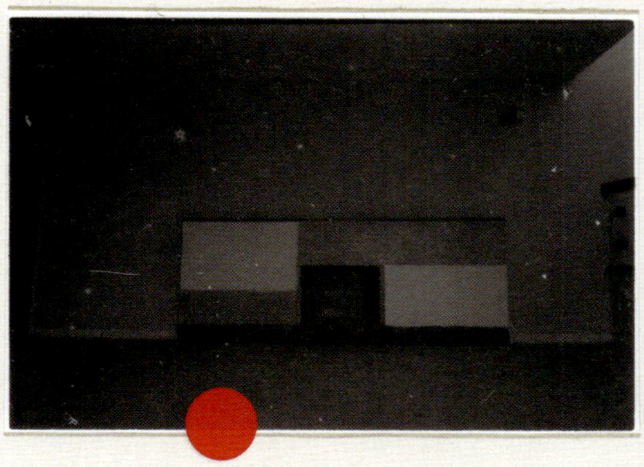

11

12

13

IRQ/812/005

MOHAMMAD ABDUL WAHAB RESIDENCE 812/DI

01

02

MOHAMMAD ABDUL WAHAB RESIDENCE 812/DI

03

04

05

06

07

08

09

10

IRQ/812/005

MOHAMMAD ABDUL WAHAB RESIDENCE

812/DI

11

12

13

14

15

16

17

18

18

20

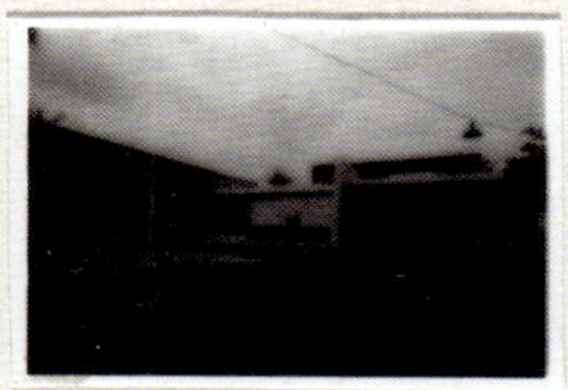
21

22.

O294ch/IRQ/812/5 (C)

IRQ/812/006

HASSAN KIRBASS RESIDENCE

812/B

01

02

03

04

05

06

1953. Mr HASSAN KIRBASS RESIDENCE 812/B

01

02

IRQ/812/007

MUDHAFFAR RESIDENCE 812/A

01

02

03

04

05

06

07

08

09

10

11

12

MUNTHIR ABBAS RESIDENCE, 1956 IRQ/812/8

01

02

03

04

05

06

07

08

09

10

MUNTHIR ABBAS RESIDENCE, 1956

IRQ/812/8

11

12

13

14

15

16

17

18

19

20

MUNTHIR ABBAS RESIDENCE, 1956 IRQ/812/8

21

22

23

24

25

26

27

28

MUNTHIR ABBAS RESIDENCE, 1956 IRQ/812/8

29

0294ch / IRQ/ 812/8 (D)

IRQ/812/009

R. CHADIRJI RESIDENCE

IRQ/812/C

OLD RESIDENCE

01

02

03

04

05

06

07

0294ch/IRQ/812/9 (A)

ABDUL MALIK KAMIL HASSAN RESIDENCE. 1956 IRQ/812/12

01

02

03

04

05

06

07

08

0294ch/IRQ/812/12 (A)

MME. ABBOUD RESIDENCE.

IRQ/812/50.

01

02

03

04

05

06

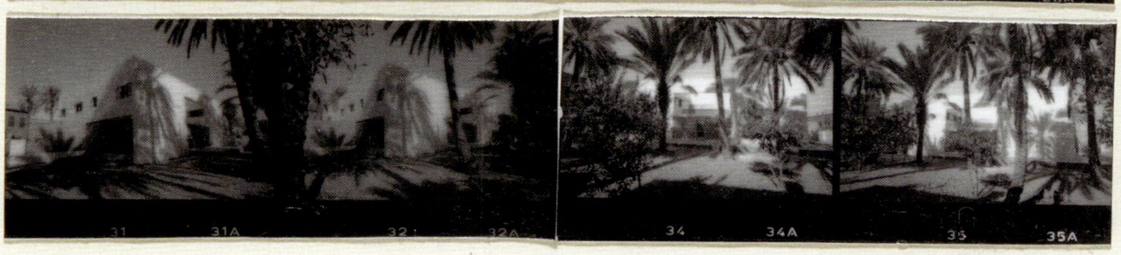

M. SHANSHAL RESIDENCE IRQ/812/90

01

02

MUHSIN
M. SHANSHAL RESIDENCE

IRQ/812/9

03

04

FAROUK AADOUSI RESIDENCE IRQ/812/110

0294ch/IRQ/8121110 (D)

H. ZAHARIA RESIDENCE

812/L
115

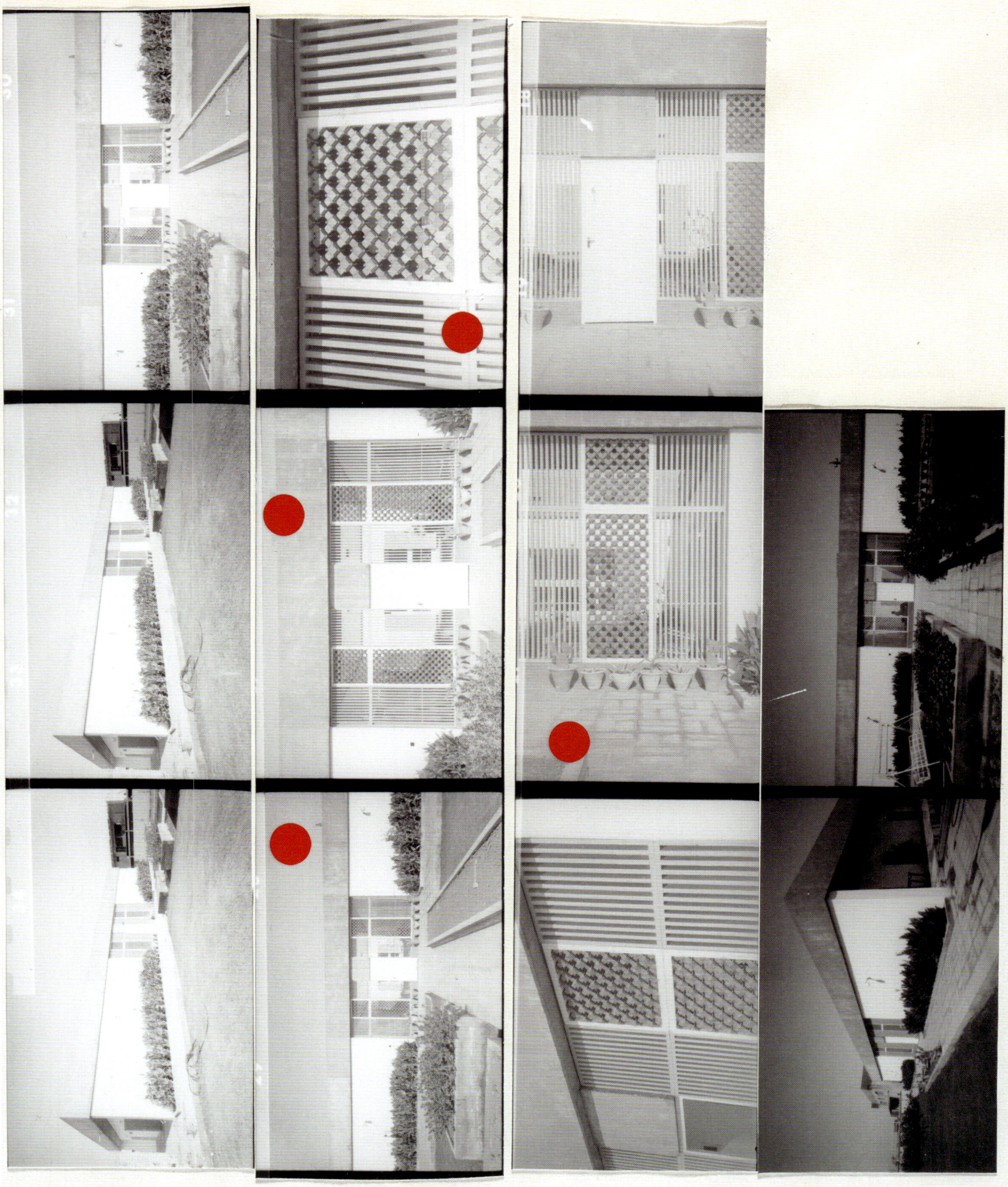

0294ch/IRQ/812/115 (A-1)

H. ZAHARIA RES.

812/L

0294ch/IRQ/812/115 (A/2)

IRQ/812/116

07

08

09

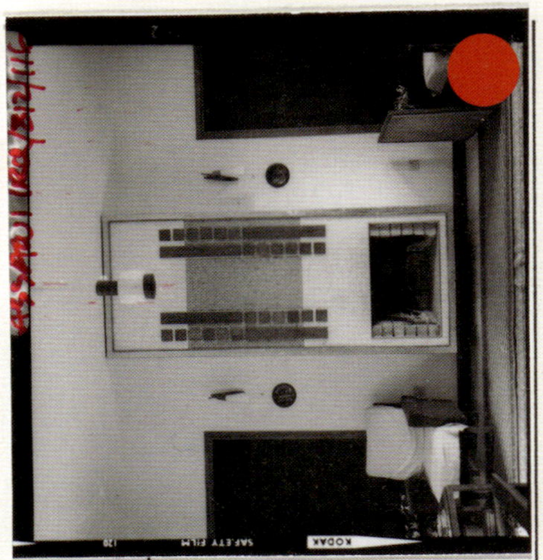

12

10

11

ASSAWI RESIDENCE IRQ/812/116

22

21

24

26

28

29

HAMOODI RESIDENCE IRQ/812/129

01

02

03

04

21
05

41
06

0294ch/IRQ/812/K29(A)

IRQ/812/130

ALBERT HANNA RESIDENCE

RL/812/- J

0294ch/IRQ/812/130 (A)

IRQ/812/130

ALBERT HANNA RESIDENCE

RL/812/- J

11

13

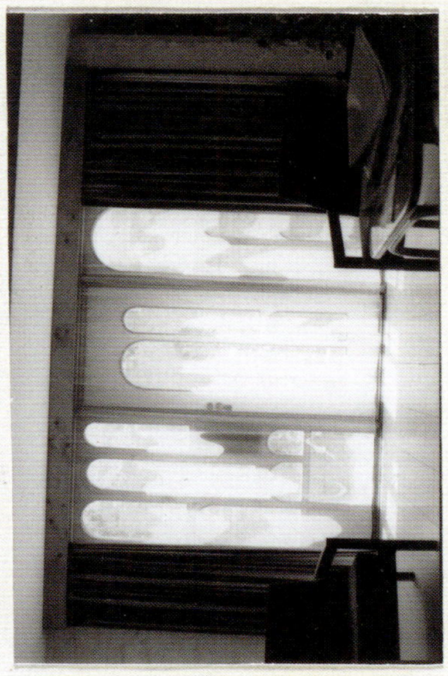

9

12

N CHADIRJI RESIDENCE

IRQ/812/G
131

YASOUB RAFIQ HOUSE IRQ/812/158 A

7

10

6

9

5

21

8

41

0294ch/IRQ/812/158(A)

61 11

12

13

71

81

0294ch/IRQ/812/158(B)

YASOUB RAFIQ HOUSE IRQ/812/158 B.

14

15

16

17

21

18

41

19

20

21

0294ch/IRQ/812/158(D)

YASOUB RAFIQ HOUSE IRQ/812/158 C.

22

23

24

25

21

26

41

27

o29uch/IRQ/812/158(E)

28

29

61

30

31

71

81

YASOUB RAFIQ HOUSE IRQ/812/158 - D

YASOUB RAFIQ HOUSE IRQ/812/158 - D

7

o29uch/IRQ/017/197(B)

IRQ/817/197

1963 MINAS RESIDENCE

IRQ/812/E

O294ch/IRQ/817/197 (A)

QAILANI RESIDENCE

812/M
216

0294ch/IRQ/812/216 (A)

MR. MUSTAPHA SHANSHAL RESIDENCE IRQ/812/218

محسن شنشل

مصطفى شنشل

MR. MUSTAPHA SHANSHAL RESIDENCE IRQ/812/218

MR AYAD HAMOOD'S RESIDENCE 1970 IRQ/812/221

02

03

MR AYAD HAMOOD'S RESIDENCE 1970 IRQ/812/221

04

05

MR AYAD HAMOOD'S RESIDENCE 1970 IRQ/812/221

06

07

08

09

MR AYAD HAMOOD'S RESIDENCE 1970 IRQ/812/221

10

11

12

MR AYAD HAMOOD'S RESIDENCE 1970 IRQ/812/221 -A

21A

5A

4A

6A

MR AYAD HAMOOD'S RESIDENCE 1970 IRQ/812/221 -A

8A

9A

10A

11A

0294ch/IRQ/812/221(K)

MR AYAD HAMOOD'S RESIDENCE IRQ/812/221 F

Film
Nº 73/001

2

6

5

21

1

3

41

Ozguch / IRQ/812/221(G)

Film
No 73/002

MR AYAD HAMOOD'S RESIDENCE IRQ/812/221 - G

0294ch/ARCH/IRQ/812/221 (A)

MR AYAD HAMOOD'S RESIDENCE IRQ/812/221

Film
N° 73/003

1

8

3.

5

2

6

21

41

0294ch/IRQ/812/221 (E)

61 7 11 10

71

81

1973 MR BAHIR FAIQ RESIDENCE IRQ/812/263

8

9

BAHIR FAIQ RESIDENCE, 1973 IRQ/812/263

BAHIR FAIQ RESIDENCE, 1973

IRQ/812/263

33

34

35

03

04

05

06

07

BAHIR FAIQ RESIDENCE, 1973 IRQ/812/263

01

02

R.CHADIRJI RESIDENCE BAGHDAD IRQ/8I2/3I2

01

03

12

IRQ/812/312

R.CHADIRJI RESIDENCE BAGHDAD IRQ/812/312

IRQ/812/312

06.+05

11.

16.+17

R.CHADIRJI RESIDENCE   BAGHDAD   IRQ/812/312

14

8

7

10

Villa Fahame

R.CHADIRJI ~~RESIDENCE~~ ~~BAGHDAD~~ IRQ/~~812~~/312

20

B+W NEGATIVE FROM COLOUR SLIDE

0294ch/IRQ/812/312(C)

IRQ/812/312

30

20

NOTE: ALL THESE COLOUR PRINTS
ARE CHEAP DIRECT PRINTS
FROM SLIDES.
CAN GET BETTER QUALITY
PRINTS.

IRQ/812/312

~~34~~ 35

36

34

IRQ/812/312

33

32

31

R.CHADIRJI RESIDENCE BAGHDAD IRQ/8I2/3I2

VILLA FAHAMA

004

CHORBICHI BUILDING - BAGHDAD IRQ/818/D

01

02

03

04

CHORBICHI BUILDING - BAGHDAD

IRQ/818/D

05

06

07

08

09

10

11

12

13

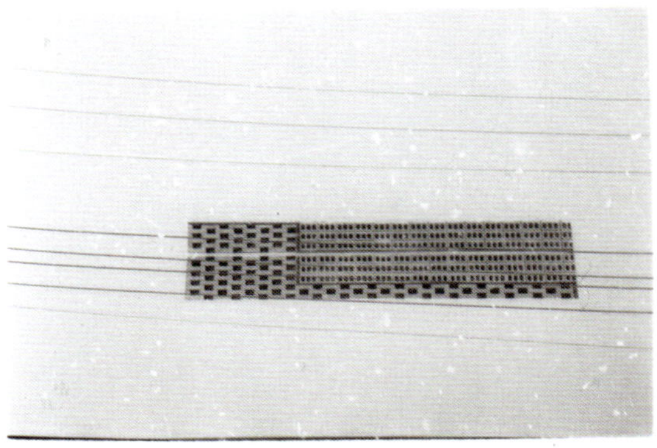
14

0294ch/IRQ/812/4 (B)

MUNIR ABBAS BUILDING

IRQ/818/11

03

04

05

06

07

08

09

10

0294ch/IRQ/818/11 (A)

MUNIR ABBAS BUILDING

IRQ/818/12

02

03

04

05

06

07

08

09

10

11.

MUNIR ABBAS BUILDING

IRQ/~~818~~/13

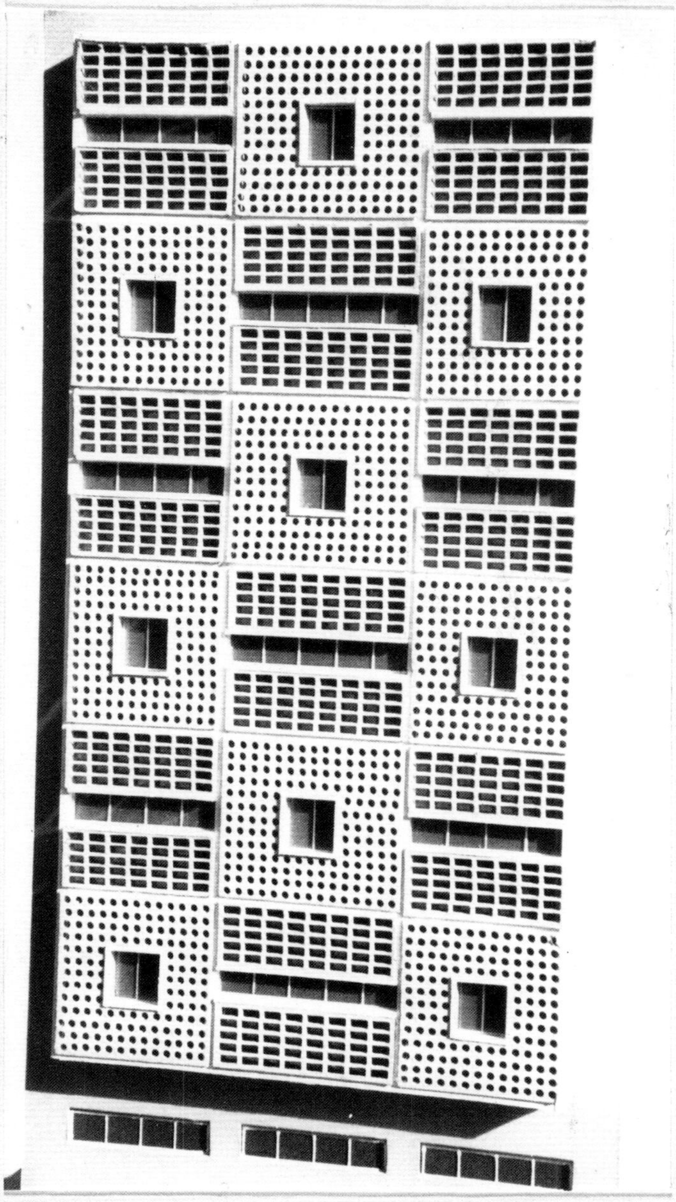

05

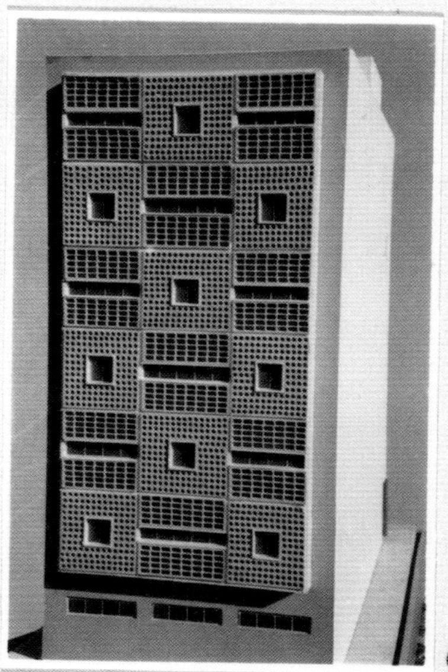

06

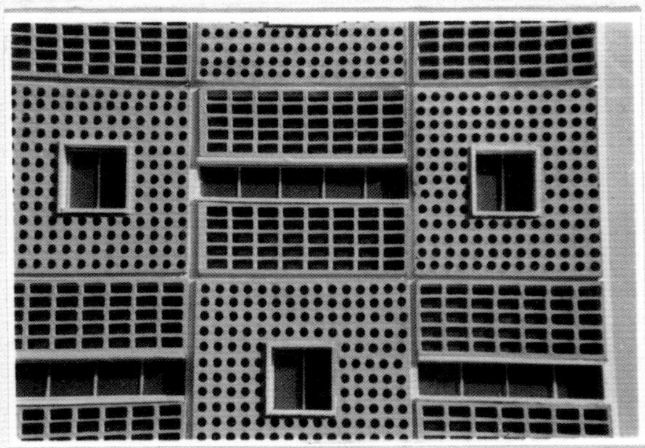

07

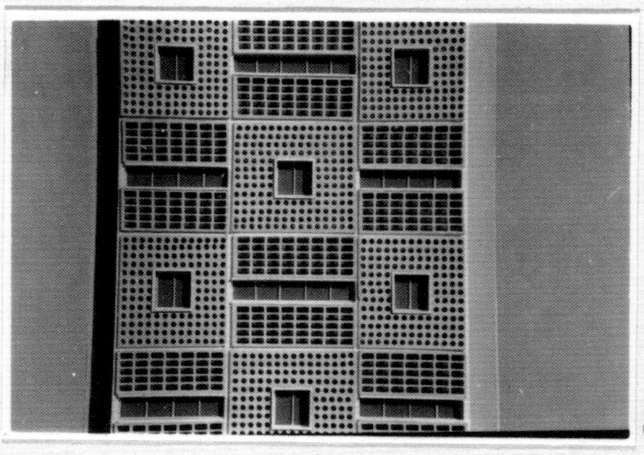

08

818/030

SHANSHAL'S HOUSING IRQ/812/

01

02

03

04

05

06

07

08

09

"RASHAD CITY" PROJECT IRQ/82/88

01

02

03

04

05

06

07

08

"RASHAD CITY" PROJECT IRQ/82/88

09

10

11

12

13

14

15

0294ch/IRQ/82/88(D)

16

17

18

19

20

21

22

23

0294ch/IRQ/82/88 (A)

"RASHAD CITY" PROJECT IRQ/82/88

24

25

26

27

28

29

30

31

32

34

35

0294ch/IRQ/82/88 (E)

850

CEMENT FACTORY HOUSING IRQ/~~27~~/109

2

3

4

5

6

7

12.

12a

13

14

13/14

15

Jarn Yafour Police Station 381/244 DHB/383

Jarn Yafour Police Station 381/244 DHB/383

O294ch/DHB/381/244 (A)

244

Jarn Yafour Police Station

DHB/383/

Al Aowha Police Station

DHB/383/261

.0294ch/DHB/383/261 (B)

Al Aowha Police Station DHB/383/261

Al Aowha Police Station DHB/383/261

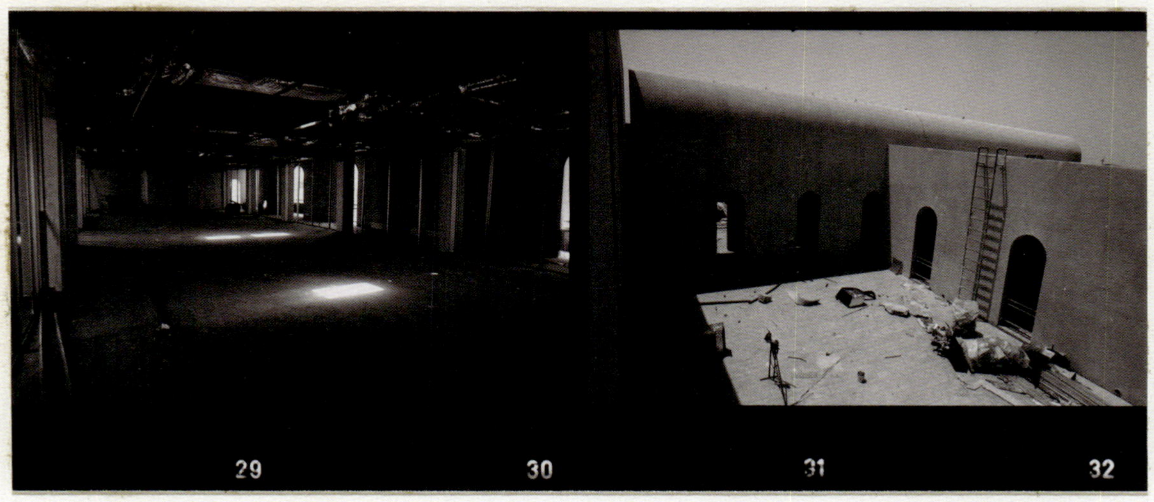

Al Aowha Police Station

Madinat Zaid Police Station

S332B

DHB/383/250

X

P.S. Madinat Zaid

مدينة زايد

0294ch/DHB/383/250(C)

Madinet Zaid Police Station

S332 B.

0294ch/DHB/383/250(B)

Al Maqta Police station

DHB/383/261

S332A

Al Maqta Police Station

DHB/383/25-1

Maqtaa P. S.

S332A

Al maqta Police Station

DMB/383/25-1

X

0294ch/DHB/383/250 (E)

S332 A

Al Maqta Police Station

DHB/383/251

0294ch/DHB/383/250(D)

NATIONAL THEATER - ABU DHABI 1977

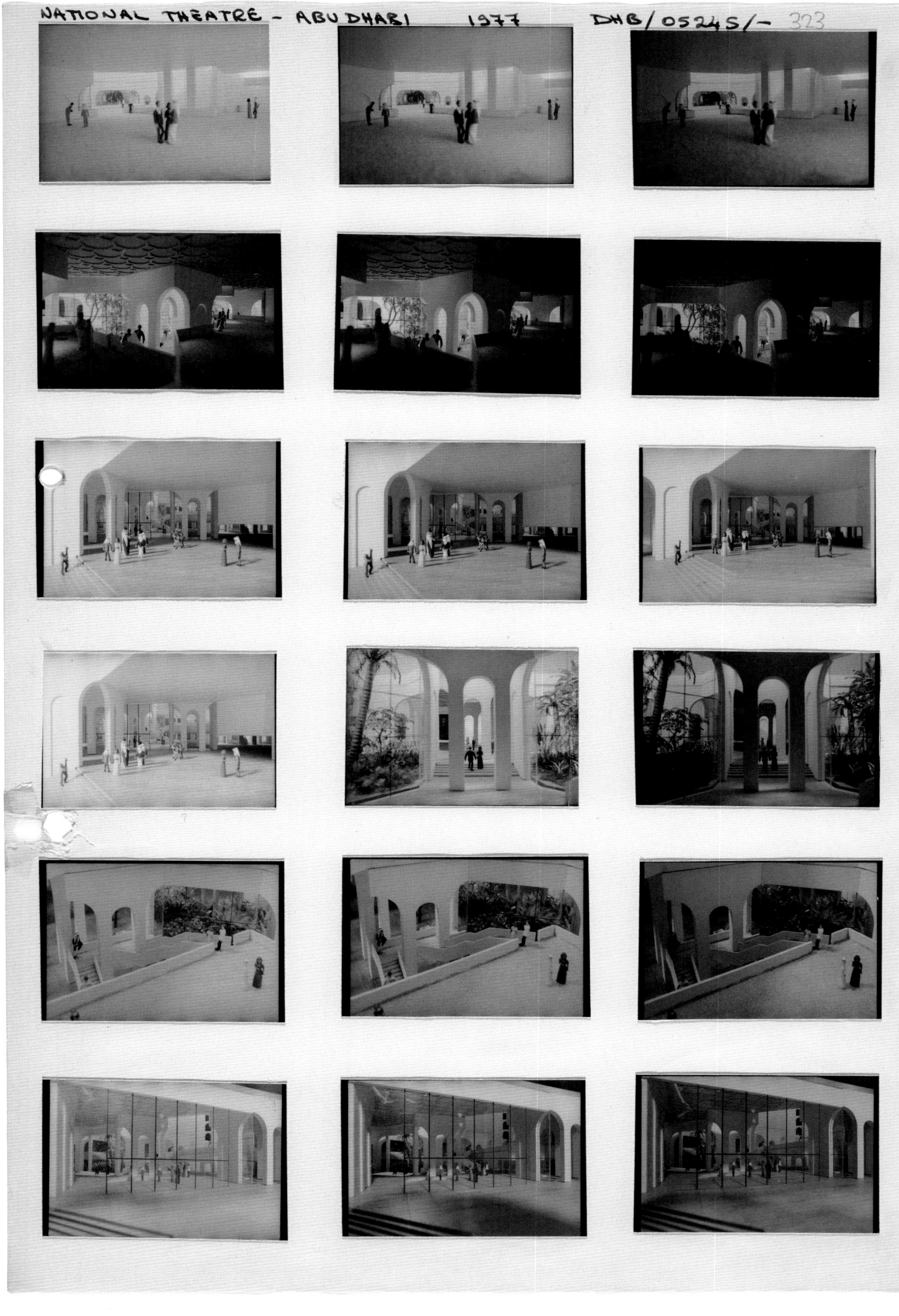
NATIONAL THEATRE - ABU DHABI 1977 DHB/05245/- 323

5332 B.

818/2 49 DHB/818/ A

Al Neami Building.

5332C

al Naeemi Build.

النعيمي

Ahmed Ghanem Al Mazroy Building

252 S332B

DHB/818/B

Mazroui Bldg

Hazza Al-Darmaki Building

253 5332 B

DHB/818/C

Al Darmaki
Residential

Mohd. Bin Sabha Building

S332A

DHB/818/~~308~~ 307

محمد بن صبحة

BEN SABHA B

0294ch/DHB/818/307 (A)

S332 C

Mohd. Bin Sabha Building

Bin Sabha B.

M.S. Al Badi Building "Al Ain" DHB/818/308

al Badi Building
(al ain city)

S332 B
DHB/818/308

Saif & Al Badi Buildings 1

32

33

35

36

Al Badi Buildi (1st. B.)
Saif bin maya

0294ch/DHB/818/308(A)

S. Al Badi Building 2

S332A

DHB/818/308

Al Badi Building (2nd Building)

Abu Dhabi

BAHRAIN FLOURMILL, 1969 BRN/273/175

HOUSING & COMMERCIAL COMPLEX FOR SHEIKH KHALIFA BIN SALMAN AL KHALIFA BRN/320/190

HOUSING & COMMERCIAL COMPLEX FOR SHEIKH KHALIFA BIN SALMAN AL KHALIFA BRN/320/190

1968 ANDALUS CINEMA - BAHRAIN BRN/525/173

1A

2A

1968 ANDULUS CINEMA - BAHRAIN BRN/525/173

12A

13A

1968 ANDULUS CINEMA - BAHRAIN BRN/525/173

14A

15A

1968 ANDULUS CINEMA - BAHRAIN BRN/525/173

18A

19A

oza4ch/BRN/525/173(G)

MR M AL HAMAD'S RESIDENCE 1967 KWT/812/163

IRQ/812/163 Neg.: 26A

MR M AL HAMAD'S RESIDENCE 1967 KWT/812/163

0294ch/KWT/812/163(A)

1970 HASSAWI'S HOUSING COMPLEX - AL HAWALLI KWT/818/176

HASSAWI BLG KUWAIT KWT/81/176

23

22

21

41

0294ch/KWT/811/176 (D)

1970 HASSAWI BUILDINGS - SALMIYAH KWT/818/181

The project titles, codes, and serial numbers typed on the Building Index sheets are frequently crossed out and corrected by hand. When compared to other sources, several discrepancies appear —different titles, dates, and numbers are sometimes given to the same project.

The following list cites three different reference systems. The first line reproduces the available inscriptions present on the sheets, including entries that have been deleted and amended. The second line contains all the available information drawn from a master index list including the file number—1 through 24—to which different sheets belong. The third line, when available, references the building titles and dates as they appear in Chadirji's book *Concepts and Influences: Towards a Regionalized International Architecture 1952-1978.*

This list cites the projects in ascending order based on the first 2 digits of the reference number inscribed on the sheet itself.

Page	Project	Year	Reference	File
pp. 03-06	Bridge		IRQ/18	
pp. 07-10	*Untitled*	1969	IRQ/18/182	
	Monument for Workers' training Campus in Waziriyah designed by Maath Alousi	1969	IRQ/984/182	2
pp. 11-12	*Untitled*		IRQ/188/188	
	Monument for Worker's Housing Scheme, Fudailiyah, Baghdad	1969	IRQ/984/188	2
	Monument in Housing Scheme, Ministry of Social Affairs, Baghdad	1969		
pp. 13-20	Flour Mill		IRQ/273/161 ~~277/159~~	
	Iraq Flour Mill Company	1967	IRQ/273/161	3
pp. 21-22	Kufa Cement Factory	1970-71	IRQ/277/187	
	Kufa Cement Factory, auxiliary buildings. Kufa	1970-71	IRQ/277/187	3
pp. 23-30	Tobacco Monopoly – Administration	1961	IRQ/31/107	
	Tobacco Monopoly, Administration. Baghdad	1961	IRQ/314/107	4
pp. 31-40	Institute of Ministry of Social Affairs. Baghdad	1969	IRQ/312/179 - IRQ/314/179	
	Administration and Training Institute for the Ministry of Social Affairs. Baghdad	1969	IRQ/314/179	4
pp. 41-42	Council of Ministers Building. Baghdad		IRQ/313/302	
	Reference is not available in Chadirji's master index			
	Administration Complex, Council of Ministers, Government of Iraq. Baghdad	1975		
pp. 43-44	Labour Trade Union Building	1973	IRQ/314/233	
	Labour Trade Union Building	1973	IRQ/314/233	6
pp. 45-62	Central Post, Telegraph & Telephone Offices	1970-1975	IRQ/315/186	
	Central Post, Telegraph & Telephone Offices. Baghdad	1970-1975	IRQ/315/186	6
	Offices, Central Post, Telegraph and Telephone Administration. Baghdad.	1971		
pp. 63-68	~~Munir Abbas Building~~ Pier Dawood Building		IRQ/320/017 ~~818/9~~	
	Pier Dawood Waqaf Building	1955	IRQ/320/017	08
pp. 68-82	Iraq Consult Office I.Q.C.	1965	IRQ/32/127	
	I.Q.C Consult Offices. Baghdad	1965	IRQ/332/127	8
	I.Q.C Consult Bureau. Baghdad	1965		
pp. 83-96	National Insurance Company. Mosul	1969	IRQ/320/151	
	National Insurance Company. Mosul	1969	IRQ/338/151	9
pp. 97-104	Federation of Industries Building	1966	IRQ/32/153	
	Federation of Industries Building. Baghdad	1966	IRQ/314/153	8
	Administration Offices Federation of Industries. Baghdad	1966		
pp. 105-106	Ruhoon Bank		IRQ/328/16	
	Ruhoon Bank	1956	IRQ/338/016	10
pp. 107-108	Rafidain Bank – Sinak Branch	1961	IRQ/328/108	
	Rafidain Bank – Sinak Branch. Baghdad	1961	IRQ/338/108	10
pp. 109-110	Rafidain Bank – Salhiyah Branch	1970	IRQ/328/165	
	Rafidain Bank – Salhiyah Branch. Baghdad	1970	IRQ/338/165	10
pp. 111-118	Commercial Bank – Mansour	1970	IRQ/328/170	
	Commercial Bank – Mansour Branch. Baghdad	1968	IRQ/338/170	11
	Branch Office, Rafidain Bank, Baghdad	1969		

pp. 119-120	Hamed Office Building		IRQ/32 - 331/011	
	Hamed Building	1954	IRQ/331/011	8
pp. 121-122	Munir Abbas Buiding		IRQ/331/013 - ~~IRQ/818/14~~	
pp. 123-124	~~Munir Abbas Building~~. *Al Arman**		IRQ/331/013 - IRQ/818/10	
pp. 125-126	Munir Abbas Buiding		IRQ/331/013 - IRQ/818/13	
pp. 127-128	Abboud Building		IRQ/3/26	
	Abboud Building	1955	IRQ/331/26	4
pp. 129-132	Waqaf Building – Alwiyah	1969	IRQ/331/195 ~~320~~	
	Waqaf Building – Alwiyah Branch. Baghdad	1969	IRQ/331/195	10
	Commercial Building, Directorate-General of the Waqaf Administration. Baghdad			
pp. 133-146	Tobacco Monopoly - Offices and Store	1966	IRQ/34/154	
	Tobacco Monopoly - Offices and Store. Baghdad	1966	IRQ/314/154	11
	Offices and stores, Tobacco Monopoly Administration. Baghdad			
pp. 147-148	Building for Hidaib Mamood		IRQ/342/66 - IRQ/331/066	
	Building for Hidaib Mamood	1957	IRQ/331/066	1
pp. 149-150	Arbil Orphanage		IRQ/446/~~166~~	
	Orphanage Centre, Arbil		IRQ/446/166	13
pp. 151-158	Veterinary College	1965	IRQ/72/103	
	Veterinary College. Baghdad	1965	IRQ/720/103	16
	Veterinary College. Baghdad University. Baghdad			
pp. 159-183	Iraq Scientific Academy	1965	IRQ/731/104	
	Iraqi Scientific Academy	1965	IRQ/731/104	17
pp. 185-186	Chemical Laboratories – *Al Mujamaa al Elmi Al Kurdi**	1967	IRQ/731/~~180~~	
	Chemical Laboratories	1967	IRQ/732/180	17
	Chemical Laboratories, Ministry of Agriculture, Baghdad	1967		
pp. 187-188	Maath Alousi's House		IRQ/812/R	
	Maath Alousi Residence		IRQ/812/	18
pp. 189-192	Hussain Jamil Residence	1955	IRQ/812/3	
	Hussain Jamil Residence	1953	IRQ/812/003	21
pp. 193-198	Mohammad Abdel Wahab Residence		IRQ/812/D1 - IRQ/812/005	
	Mohammad Abdel Wahab Residence	1953	IRQ/812/005	18
pp. 199-202	Hassan Kirbass Residence		IRQ/812/B - IRQ/812/006	
	Hassan Kirbassi Residence	1953	IRQ/812/006	18
pp. 203-204	Mudhaffar Residence		IRQ/812/A - IRQ/812/007	
	Ali Mudhaffer Residence	1954	IRQ/812/007	18
pp. 205-212	Munthir Abbas Residence	1956	IRQ/812/8	
	Munthir Abbas Residence	1955	IRQ/812/008	21
pp. 213-214	R. Chadirji Old Residence		IRQ/812/C - IRQ/812/009	
	R. Chadirji Residence. (Conversion of stables)	1954	IRQ/812/009	18

* Translated from Arabic

pp. 215-216	Abdul Malik Kamil Hassan Residence	1956	IRQ/812/12	
	Abdul Malik Kamil Hassan Residence	1956	IRQ/812/012	22
pp. 217-218	Mme Abboud Residence		IRQ/812/050	
	Mme Abboud Residence	1959	IRQ/812/050	22
pp. 219-222	Muhsin Shanshal Residence		IRQ/812/090 ~~218~~	
	Muhsin Shanshal Residence	1960	IRQ/812/090	20
pp. 223-224	Farouk Alousi Residence		IRQ/812/110	
	Dr. Faroul al Alousi Residence	1961	IRQ/812/110	19
pp. 225-228	H. Zaharia Residence		IRQ/812/L - 115	
	H. Zakharia Residence	1962	IRQ/812/115	18
pp. 229-230	Assawi Residence		IRQ/812/116	
	A. H. Azzawi Residence	1962	IRQ/812/116	19
pp. 231-232	Hamoodi Residence		IRQ/812/129	
	Hamoodi Residence	1965	IRQ/812/129	18
pp. 233-236	Albert Hanna Residence		IRQ/812/J - IRQ/812/130	
	Albert Hanna Residence	1965	IRQ/812/130	18
pp. 237-238	N Chadirji Residence		IRQ/812/G - 131	
	N. Chadirji Residence	1962	IRQ/812/131	18
pp. 239-254	Yasoub Rafiq House	1965	IRQ/812/158	
	Yasoub Rafiq House	1965	IRQ/812/158	20
pp. 255-258	Minas Residence	1963	IRQ/812/E - IRQ/817/197	
	Minas Residence	1963	IRQ/812/197	18
pp. 259-260	Qailani Residence		IRQ/812/M - 216	
	Adnan Qailani Residence	1963	IRQ/812/216	18
pp. 261-264	Mr. Mustapha Shanshal Residence		IRQ/812/218	
	Mustapha Shanshal Residence	1963	IRQ/812/218	20
pp. 265-284	Mr. Ayad Hamood Residence	1970	IRQ/812/221	
	Mr. Ayad Hamood Residence	1970	IRQ/812/221	21
pp. 285-292	Bahir Faiq Residence	1973	IRQ/812/263	
	Bahir Faiq Residence		IRQ/812/263	21
pp. 293-308	R. Chadirji's Residence. Baghdad. Villa Fahama		IRQ/812/312	
	R. Chadirji's Residence	1975	IRQ/812/312	21
pp. 309-312	Chorbichi Building – Baghdad		IRQ/818/004	
	Chorbachi Building – Baghdad	1953	IRQ/818/004	22
pp. 313-314	~~Munir Abbas Building~~ *Al-Hamad Building**		IRQ/818/11	
	Al-Hamad Building	1954	IRQ/331/011	08
pp. 315-318	Munir Abbas Building		IRQ/818/12 - 13	
pp. 319-320	Shanshal's Housing		IRQ/818/030	
	Shanshal's Housing Prtoject	1958	IRQ/818/030	20

* Translated from Arabic

pp. 321-330	"Rashad City" Project	1959	IRQ/82/88	
	Rashad City. Rashad	1959	IRQ/818/088	4
pp. 331-334	Cement Factory Housing		IRQ/850/109 ~~27~~	
	Cement Factory Housing	1967	IRQ/858/109	3
pp. 335-338	Jarn Yafour Police Station		DHB/381/244	
	Jarn Yafour Police Station	1977	DHB/381/244	13
pp. 339-346	Al Aowha Police Station		DHB/283/261	
	Al Aowha Police Station	1977	DHB/281/261	13
pp. 347-350	Madinat Zaid Police Station		DHB/383/250	
	Madinat Zaid Police Station	1972	DHB/381/250	13
pp. 351-358	Al Maqta Police Station		DHB/383/251	
	Maqta'a Police Station	1972	DHB/381/251	13
pp. 359-362	National Theater, Abu Dhabi	1977	DHB/05245/323	
	National Theater	1977	DHB/524/323	13
pp. 363-364	Al Neami Building		DHB/818/249	
	Al Neami Building	1972	DHB/818/249	22
pp. 365-366	Ahmed Ghanem Al Mazroy		DHB/818/252	
	Ahmed Ghanem Al Mazroy	1976	DHB/818/252	22
pp. 367-368	Hazza Al-Darmaki Building		DHB/818/253	
	Hazza Al-Darmaki Building	1975	DHB/818/253	22
pp. 369-372	Mohd. Bin Sabha Building. *Mohamad Ben Sabha**		DHB/818/307	
pp. 373-374	Al Badi Building, Al Ain City		DHB/818/308	
pp. 375-378	Saif Bin Maya and Al Badi Buildings		DHB/818/308	
pp. 379-380	Bahrain Flourmill	1969	BRN/273/175	
	Bahrain Flour Mill Project	1969	BRN/273/175	03
pp. 381-384	Housing & Commercial Complex for Sheikh Khalifa Bin Salman Al Khalifa		BRN/320/190	
	Housing & Commercial Complex for Sheikh Khalifa Bin Salman Al Khalifa		BRN/818/190	09
	Sheikh Khalifa Building (Commercial and Residential) Manama, Bahrain	1969		
pp. 385-392	Al Andalus Cinema - Bahrain	1968	BRN/525/173	
	Andalus Cinema	1968	BRN/525/173	13
pp. 393-396	Mr. M. Al Hamad's Residence	1967	KWT/812/163	
	M. Al Hamad's Residence	1967	KWT/812/163	20
	M. Hamad Residence, Kuwait	1967		
pp. 397-400	Hassawi's Housing Complex - Al Hawalli	1970	KWT/818/176	
	Hassawi's Housing Complex, Al Hawalli	1970	KWT/818/176	22
pp. 401-402	Hassawi Buildings - Salmiyah	1970	KWT/818/181	
	Hassawi Housing Complex, Salmiyah	1970	KWT/818/181	22

* Translated from Arabic